SLAVIC PEOPLES

SLAVIC PEOPLES

BY THOMAS CALDECOT CHUBB

Illustrated by W. T. Mars

SHELBY COUNTY
LIBRARY

THE WORLD PUBLISHING COMPANY

Cleveland and New York

To Frances and René Pingeon

and their children

Published by The World Publishing Company
2231 West 110th Street, Cleveland 2, Ohio

Published simultaneously in Canada by
Nelson, Foster & Scott Ltd.

Library of Congress Catalog Card Number: 62-10244

CONTENTS

*Pronunciations for unfamiliar words
are given in the Index*

FROM THE LAND OF
GOG AND MAGOG

In 860—more than 1,100 years ago—the twenty-one-year-old Byzantine emperor, Michael III, left his glittering capital, Constantinople, and marched proudly toward his eastern frontier.

This city—it was also called Byzantium—was located on the Bosporus, the narrow body of water which divides Europe from Asia Minor. And since the realm over which its emperor ruled extended from Sicily in one direction through the Balkans and Greece almost to Mesopotamia in the other, it was necessary for him to keep a watchful eye in every direction.

Behind him came his whole army. His powerful *cataphracts* —the heavy cavalry that served as his tank corps. The *trapezidae,* or light cavalry. The light infantry and the heavy infantry.

With him also were the *tagmata,* or regiments usually stationed in the city to aid its garrison in defending the God-guarded metropolis. Missing only was the Byzantine navy. This was an overland expedition.

As the long serpentlike file moved slowly across the lofty highland which today is modern Turkey, Michael's mind was fixed upon his purpose.

This was to make his Byzantine Empire feared and respected again.

It greatly needed this. For not only had it been torn by riots and revolution and racked by religious quarrels, but a new foreign enemy had begun to press in from the south as well. The desert Arabs, now united by the teachings of Mohammed!

These camel-riding warriors had already marched right up to the shores of the Bosporus, and this very spring the turbaned soldiers of the caliph had captured a key stronghold in a mountain pass which protected Byzantium from the southeast. They had taken prisoner the important well-fed Byzantine aristocrat who defended it.

To be sure, they had exchanged him within a month. But exchanging a prisoner was not enough.

"These enemies of God must be crushed utterly!" cried Michael. "They must be torn out root and branch! They must be sent back to Satan, who spawned them!"

Presently he could see ahead of him the snow-crowned peaks of Cappadocia. At their foot was a mighty stream, the ancient Halys, now the Kizil Irmak. Into it ran a swift tributary, the Mauropotamos.

On its far bank was the infidel army. The sun flashed on its curved scimitars.

The moment had come!

But as Michael was debating as to how to move his army across to meet the Moslems, a messenger rode up at a gallop. His tidings were the tidings of the prophet Ezekiel.

"Set thy face toward Gog and the land of Magog, the prince of Rosh, Mesheck, and Jubal. Out of the uttermost parts of the north shalt come a great company, and a mighty army and every wall shall fall to the ground."

Then he delivered the message of the *eparch*, or governor, of Constantinople.

"The bloody race of the Scythians, the so-called Ros, have come through the Euxine (the Black Sea) to the Stenon (the Bosporus). They have plundered all the palaces and monasteries. They have carried off all the sacred vessels and all the property."

They had even raided the island of Terebinth, almost in sight of the city, and the home of the exiled patriarch Ignatius.

"They seized twenty-two of his servants and cut them to pieces with axes on the sterns of their ships."

The city, the messenger reported, was in near panic.

"Where," had cried Photius, the new patriarch, "is the Christ-loving emperor? Where are arms, machines, military counsels, equipment?

"Ruin," he went on, "and slaughter confront us. I see a savage people surround the city and plunder the suburbs. They destroy everything; they lay everything waste. They are like locusts in a cornfield, like rot on the vines, or like a hurricane or a typhoon or a flood. And their cruelty has not confined itself to human beings. They have destroyed dumb animals—not only horses and oxen but even helpless fowl."

Here is what actually had happened.

The night of June 17, 860, was wild and stormy with heavy rains and gusty winds. But the next day dawned clear and calm, and as the Byzantines looked down from their city, they

saw beneath them a fleet of long, lean vessels. They were two hundred in number, and on board were twenty thousand men, most of whom had light blond hair, and many of whom had green or sharp gray eyes.

The rank and file were bearded, but the leaders had shaven chins and long mustaches. Above coats of mail, many of them wore brightly colored cloaks whose corners were fastened at the shoulders with gold or silver buckles. Some of them carried bows and arrows. Others carried a spear, an ax, or a sword with a broad double-edged blade. The sun glittered from their weapons.

Suddenly a shout arose. "Perun! Gromovik Perun! Perun!" "Volos! Volos! Perun! Volos!"

Then the barbarians from the north launched the attack.

They did not take the city, however. Its walls were too thick and too high, and the Byzantines were experienced with invaders who were strong and brave but who knew very little about carrying on a siege. Michael, too, realized that these golden-haired men were even more dangerous than the Arabs were. He returned as swiftly as possible. He and his army slipped through the encircling enemies and joined the defenders. The *eparch* could now keep the adversary at bay.

But if they could not take Constantinople, these warriors who had come so suddenly were only defeated by a miracle.

In the winter of 861 when the invaders ringed the walls for more than half a year, the emperor, along with the patriarch and an array of brocaded church functionaries and important court officials, paraded solemnly to the Church of Our Lady of Blachernae in the northwestern corner of the city. There they prayed all night, singing hymns and intoning the most sonorous passages of their liturgy. In the morning they went in solemn procession to the shores of the narrow Golden Horn.

"Intercede for us, O Theotokos!" they implored. "Help us, O Virgin Mary!"

They then dipped her consecrated vestments into the water.

The Black Sea has been given its very name of "black" or "evil" because of the icy storm winds which sweep it, particularly in the months of January, February, and March. But not even its reputation could account for the prompt answer.

As the emperor and his patriarch prayed and paraded, the

waters were like a flat mirror. But hardly had they finished speaking when a gale smote without warning. Caught unprepared, most of the enemy vessels were dashed upon the hostile shore. There they broke to pieces. A large part of the fighting men—and even many of the sailors—were drowned as they tried to wade ashore. Others were slain by the aroused Byzantines.

When, after a long and terrible night, the weather grew tranquil again, only a pitiful remnant had survived. These sailed off as mysteriously as they had come.

The followers of
Askold and Dir

Who were these marauders who had stormed in out of the foggy north?

What manner of people were they?

Were they indeed the sons of Gog from the land of Magog, the same warriors who had poured down from the Caucasus Mountains in the days of the prophet?

"And when the thousand years are expired," it says in the Bible, "Satan shall be loosed out of his prison, and shall go out to deceive the nations which are in the four quarters of the earth, Gog and Magog, to gather them together to battle: the number of whom *is* as the sand of the sea."

Did they come to chasten the Byzantines for hurling down the sacred images? Some of the orthodox thought so.

Or were they just one more of the invading people who had been crashing against the gates of the empire for the past 500 years? The Huns. The Goths who came from Sweden. The yellowish Avars who lived in "rings," or fenced enclosures, one of which was thirty-eight miles in circumference. The

16

Bulgarians. And lately a new people who were called Slavonians, or sometimes Serbs, or Croats.

These and other questions were asked by the people in the great city. Who were they? Would they come again with fire and sword?

The Byzantines—and even the Greeks and Romans before them—did not have the answers. They were not scientific students of archaeology or race, and to them those who did not speak Greek or Latin were simply barbarians. No matter how civilized they were, they were still barbarians.

Only a few early historians had been more specific.

The famous Greek historian Herodotus—who was born about 484 B.C.—traveled widely in the ancient world, and among the many people he described were those who lived on the shores of a wide lake from which flowed a great river which he called the Tyras. We now know it was the Dniester in southwest Russia.

These people had snub noses and long beards. They were also, said Herodotus, practicing werewolves. Every one of them, he said, became a wolf for a few days and then became a man again. This probably means that they were wolf worshipers. They may have been cannibals. They certainly had cannibals for neighbors.

More than five hundred years later the great Roman historian Tacitus told of a similar people.

"East of the Suiones (the Swedes)," he reported, "is another sea. It is sluggish and almost motionless. We believe that it surrounds the earth, for the last radiance of the setting sun lingers on there until sunrise." The famous midnight sun! It was known even to this ancient Roman.

Beyond this sea, Tacitus continued, were a number of backward tribes. The Aestii. The Sitones. The Peucini. The Venedi. The Fenni.

We can recognize at least three of these tribes. The Esthonians. The Wends—or white-haired people. And the Finns.

"I do not know whether to call them Germans or Sarmatians," Tacitus admitted.

They gather amber which they called *glesum,* he said, and they marvel at the price they receive for it. The Sitones are ruled by a woman. They all live in sloth and filth.

Yet he acknowledged that at least the Venedi (the Wends) had fixed habitations, carried shields, and delighted in fleetness of foot.

Another five hundred years later, a famous historian described two other northern tribes. Procopius of Caesaria served as secretary to the great Byzantine general Belisarius, and as he went with him on his various campaigns he often described many of the things he saw.

North of the Ister (the Danube), he reported—but they occasionally cross it in quest of plunder—live two nations called the Antae and the Sklavenoi. They occupy vast lands, or at any rate, wide empty spaces. From ancient of days they have had the same institutions and customs. They speak the same language. Although they have two names, they are really but a single people.

Then he proceeded to set down these common customs.

"They are not ruled by one man," he said, "but live under a democracy. They believe that one god, the master of the lightning, is the lord of all things, and they sacrifice to him cattle and other victims. They do not believe in fate, however, nor that it has any power among men. Yet when death threatens them either through sickness or through war, they promise that they will sacrifice to this fate in which they do not believe, and if they escape unharmed, they keep this promise. They also worship rivers and nymphs.

"They are hardy," he added. "They are tall and stalwart. They are neither very blond nor are they very dark, but instead they are all slightly reddish in color. They live a rough, hard life, giving no thought to bodily comfort."

He then finished up with two phrases which make us think of Tacitus's comment about the barbarian east Baltic tribes.

"They are like the Massagetae." (The Massagetae were a repulsive nomad people who lived near the Aral Sea and supposedly ate their own parents.) "They are continually and at all times covered with uncleanness!"

But it was not until one hundred years after the attack on Constantinople that somebody wrote down something which sums up just who the attackers from the north really were.

At that time a German emperor, Otto, sent Liutprand of Cremona as his ambassador to the Byzantine emperor, Nicephorus Phocas. The bishop was a very fussy Italian who spent most of his time complaining about Greek (the Western people called the Byzantines Greeks) food—especially the garlic-seasoned Greek fish sauce—and also about the shabby treatment he received. But when he wasn't complaining, he too looked and listened very carefully, and wrote down what he saw and heard.

This is one of the things he wrote down.

"The city of Constantinople has to the north of it the Hungarians, the Patzinaks, the Russians, and the Bulgarians."

"The latter live too close for my taste," he added.

He had a personal grudge against the Bulgarians!

Then he set out to describe one of these peoples.

They come from the regions of the North Wind, he explained, and the Greeks call them Rusii, or the Ruddy Ones.

"We, however, prefer to call them the Nordmanni, or the Northmen."

Almost by accident Bishop Liutprand had stumbled on the truth.

For the men who had attacked the city were both Northmen and Rusii.

The two leaders of the expedition (their names were Askold and Dir) were indeed Northmen, vikings, or Varangians as they were also called. They were chieftains under Rurik, who only a few years earlier at Novgorod in the north had established the first Russian state. But the men who followed them—or at least a great many of them—were not vikings at all. They belonged to an entirely different people.

Almost three hundred years after the events we have related, the aging prior of a Russian monastery scratched out the history of his nation.

"After the flood," old Sylvester wrote, "the sons of Noah divided up the earth among them."

To the lot of Shem (and we now speak of the Semitic people) fell the Orient—from Phoenicia and from Araby the Blest to distant India.

To the lot of Ham fell the southern regions—from Mauretania and the island of Sardinia to Libya and Numidia and to the river Gihon. The river Gihon is the one we call the Nile.

"But to the lot of Japheth," he continued, "fell the northern and the western sections.

"For the following nations are among those who are the race of Japheth. The Varangians. The Swedes. The Normans. The Gotlanders. The English. The Spaniards. The Italians. The Romans. The Germans. The French. The Venetians. The Genoese. And many others."

The Rusii too! The Russians! Or the Ros!

"Certain of these sons of Japheth came to settle by the Don, by the Vistula, by the Dvina, by the Dnieper, by the Dniester, and by the Volga," Sylvester continued.

(These are the mighty rivers of Poland, the Ukraine, and modern Russia. One of them, the Volga, is as long, or almost as long, as the Mississippi.)

Three brothers from one of these wandering tribes found a wooded hilltop at a bend of the Dniester, and there they built a village. They named it Kiev after the oldest brother.

Because it was at a convenient point for men coming from the north and south, it became prosperous.

Because it had become prosperous, it was attacked.

The attackers were the Khazars, a nomad nation related to the Turks.

The Khazars demanded tribute. "One white squirrel skin from every hearth!" they demanded.

These they could sell to the Persians or the Byzantines.

But the men of Kiev had heard of the vikings who were already protecting their kinsmen to the north of them. "Help us too!" they implored.

Askold and Dir agreed to do this. With their *druzhina,* or small band of personal fighting men, they left northern Novgorod and marched to the city on the great river.

Soon they were the rulers of Kiev, and the men of Kiev became their followers.

It was these men of Kiev, now under viking leadership—
they called themselves Polyanians—who portaged their frail
monoxyla (boats hollowed out of a single log) around the
noisy Dniester rapids and then drifted downward to the distant
mouth. There they built or found true viking ships. It was
these men who attacked the fabled city of Constantinople in
860.

They were Slavic tribesmen who would one day become one
of the many Slavic nations. They were a part of the so-called
Glory People.

(According to legend, the name *Slav* comes from the word
slava, which means "glory" in most Slavic languages. But
some say it comes from *slobo,* or "speech." Hence, the Slavs,
in their own opinion, were the people who talked something
you could understand, as opposed to the Nemsky—the Noth-
ing-sayers, or speakers of gibberish—which was the Slavic
name for the Germans.)

There is at least a possibility that they were related to the
men with snub noses and long beards described by Herodotus.
They were certainly related to Tacitus's Venedi-Wends—and
perhaps to his Sitones and Peucini, but not to his Fenni, and
only distantly, if at all, to his Aestii. They were at least cousins
to the Antae and the Sklavenoi. They were at least partly of
the same blood as Bishop Liutprand's despised Bulgarians.

Even in those days, the Slavic people had spread widely
through middle Europe. Slavic tribes or nations occupied all
of what is now Germany (Berlin gets its very name from *berlo,*
an old Slav word for "piling" or "post"); all of modern Poland; all of modern Czechoslovakia; much of modern Hungary; some of modern Austria; much of modern Romania; and
almost all of European Russia.

In the Balkans, there were Slavs in most of present-day Bulgaria and Yugoslavia, and they had also reached the very walls of Athens and crossed the Isthmus of Corinth. Some of them may even have sailed over the blue Aegean to Asia Minor and Crete.

Today, the Slavic people dwell in an even larger domain. To be sure, the Germans and others drove them out of much of central Europe during the Middle Ages. But to make up for this loss, Slavic pioneers, fur traders, and adventurers pushed their way eastward over the Ural Mountains and then across the tundra to the Pacific. Long before Kit Carson, or even Lewis and Clark, had opened up the Western United States, Russians like Stroganov, who was a nobleman, or like the wild Cossak, Yermak, "a blue-eyed giant with a golden beard" who had been condemned to death for stealing horses, or like Semyen Dezhnev, the sable hunter turned explorer, advanced slowly—it took them a century to do it—until they came to the end of the continent. They crossed rivers like the Yenisei and the Lena frozen from the bottom up. Sometimes they did battle with the Samoyeds and Yakuts of Siberia. And they always did battle with the weather. Finally they reached the Bering Strait and could see North America across the glint of ice.

At one time the Slavs went even farther. Russian settlers moved into Alaska, which they held until Russia sold it to the United States in 1867. Some of the more adventurous Russians even explored northern California where there is still a Russian River.

In the opposite direction more than ten thousand miles and more than 180 degrees of latitude away—more than halfway around the world—there are Slavs too. From the little ports of

Dalmatia, across the Adriatic Sea from Italy, other men set sail. They seek sardine, herring, or tunny instead of whale, walrus, and seal. They are Yugoslavs, not Russians. They are dark-complexioned, not ruddy or blond. But they use the same words for wind and for sea, and the same words for cloud and for sky. They are brothers—and not too far under the skin.

The northern and southern extent of the lands occupied by Slavs is almost as great. At Cape Chelyuskin, which is the northernmost point of Asia, and at a place called Verkhoyansk, where the temperature has fallen to 95 degrees below zero and where the permafrost—the frost which does not thaw out even in summer—is more than 100 feet deep, the settlers and the men who run the lumber mills are Slavs.

But the sun bathers in the Crimea with its fig trees and its oleanders are also Slavs.

The Montenegrin sheepherder, who only a few decades ago (I have seen this myself) perched on the bare hillside, carrying a long rifle and wearing either a white kilt or baggy white trousers, is a Slav.

So is the Polish peasant who patiently plants rye and potatoes as his ancestors have done for generations.

So is the skilled Czech artisan.

So too is the Bulgarian who in a fragrant and sunny valley hemmed in by the mighty Balkan Mountains still grows the flowers out of which attar of roses is distilled. This is the basis of almost every expensive perfume in the world.

Other Slavs live in the United States and in many other lands, from Germany and Austria and France to far Australia. Louis Adamic, an American writer of Slav origin, relates how in a little Yugoslav village high in the hills, he met men who had helped build the Empire State building in New York. But many Slavs stayed in the United States where they became statesmen and scientists and businessmen and famous athletes and just good citizens.

Obviously the Slavs have also greatly grown in number.

In the days of Askold and Dir, they were scattered tribes-men spread over a wide and thinly populated country. Today the Slavic-speaking peoples number 284 million. In Europe, more people speak a Slavic tongue than any other language. Taking the world as a whole, only the languages of China and perhaps the combined languages of India, are spoken by more people.

Of course, such a numerous people, scattered so widely, could not be all alike. There are tall Slavs—like those near the Bocche di Cattaro in Yugoslavia where the average male height is six foot three. There are short Slavs like those in Po-land and in parts of Russia. There are dark Slavs and light ones and ones who are in between.

Similarly, the Slavs have different kinds of temperament. The fiery Balkan revolutionist of the past century was a typical Slav, but the patient, hard-working peasant who makes up the largest percentage of the population of most Slav countries is also typical.

Nor do the Slavs have the same kind of backgrounds or the same history.

But when all this is taken into consideration and when every kind of allowance is made, the Slavs do have a single basic culture, and this culture has been very important to us.

What it is and how it came to be is not easy to explain be-cause the story takes place over so many years and involves so many peoples and events. Let us begin at the beginning.

IN THE BEGINNING

In the very earliest days—but long after there had been men resembling apes, or apes resembling men in several other parts of the world—the continent of Europe did not have a single human being on it. To be sure, there were various kinds of animals, although not all were the same species as today, and the sky must have known the flight of birds. But there was not a single man.

Then *Pithecanthropus* put in an appearance. At least a million years ago, and as far north as England, he chipped or flaked stones into crude instruments, and may even have begun to speak.

Ape-man (for that is what *Pithecanthropus* means) was followed by man himself, and then by *Homo sapiens,* which is our kind of man. *Homo sapiens* included Heidelberg man, who lived in Germany and elsewhere; and Neanderthal man with his shuffling gait, his big head, and his thick bull neck; and the handsome, artistic Cro-Magnon whose red-and-black paintings can still be seen on the walls of caves in Spain and southern France.

None of these people were our true ancestors, although it is just possible that the Cro-Magnons and perhaps even some of the Neanderthals may have intermarried with their successors. But they were soon followed by a new group (or by new groups, for they were more than one people) who almost certainly were our ancestors.

These newcomers were short and dark, and they may have had blue eyes. It is thought that their strain still survives in Wales and western Ireland. Their language may survive in modern Basque.

They were a primitive people who lived mainly by hunting, fishing, and the gathering of food. A few of them may have understood the beginnings of agriculture, but they did not use metal, and they had no domestic animal except the dog.

But these short, dark people were not allowed to have Europe to themselves indefinitely. They were not even allowed to have it to themselves for very long. As the climate grew better and the game more plentiful, other groups moved in.

One of these was a taller, longer-headed people with ruddy complexion and red-brown, auburn, or at least chestnut hair. There is more than one theory as to where they came from, but probably it was by way of Asia Minor.

These new people were more advanced than were their smaller, darker predecessors. For one thing, they used copper and bronze. In other words, they had moved out of the Stone Age.

They drove most of the older inhabitants before them into obscure corners. But some of them they conquered and assimilated. Out of this assimilation—although in some places the red-brown people's blood remained pure or almost pure— was born a new people or a new culture group.

(We must be careful when we use the word *race*. We now know that there may be no such thing as pure race in the way we used to understand it.)

They were old Sylvester's "sons of Japheth."

Today we call them Indo-Europeans. (A majority of those of you who read this book are Indo-Europeans. You all speak an Indo-European tongue.) The Slavic people are one of the great divisions of this Indo-European group.

Until about 2500 B.C. or a little earlier, perhaps, their ancestors and the ancestors of every other Indo-European lived in a single area and all spoke a single language. Where this was we do not know, but there is much reason to believe that it was either in southern Russia or between the Black Sea and the Caspian.

But then suddenly they broke up into various peoples and separated into every direction.

As far as Europe was concerned, the first to come were the Thracians, a wild people who tattooed themselves and performed dizzying goat dances in honor of the god of wine. They settled in the eastern Balkan peninsula. Many of Alexander the Great's soldiers were their descendants.

Some three hundred years later, they were followed by the Illyrians and the Hellenes. The Illyrians were the ancestors of the modern Albanians. The Hellenes were the ancient Greeks, the people who later gave us Homer and Socrates and Plato. But in those days they were barbarians themselves.

Others of the newcoming red-brown people were the Teutons, who were so blond that the Greeks called them the *pollioi,* or gray-haired ones, and the Celts and the Italic people, some of whom became dark.

The Teutons and the Italic people went to Germany and Italy, but the Celts at first settled in Austria and Switzerland and in Bohemia. Later they made their way to Gaul, or modern France. Some of them even crossed the English Channel.

(Of course, some of the Indo-Europeans did not go to Europe at all. One group remained in the wide lands north of the Black Sea and on both sides of the Caspian. These were the Iranians. The Scythians and the Sarmatians and later the conquering Medes and Persians were the best known of the Iranian people. Others climbed the more than 14,000 feet to cross the Hindu-Kush into Kashmir and then northern India. Still others moved into Asia Minor, where they became the Hittites. The Hittites are mentioned in the Bible. King David's general, Uriah, was a Hittite.)

But there was one group of this ruddy-complexioned people who did not press southward toward the blue waters and the balmy climate of the Mediterranean. Nor did they seek relatively salubrious central or western Europe. They did not go on to India.

Instead—and it must have been about the same time that the Thracians and the Illyrians and the Hellenes moved into the Balkans—they plodded slowly and methodically toward almost as bleak and dreary an area as you could possibly find.

I cannot tell you exactly the route they traveled, but by looking at their archaeological remains and by studying their language and their customs, it is possible to make a good guess.

Almost certainly, they moved northward from the steppes. The Iranians held the steppes in those days, and we find

many Iranian words in this migrating people's language. There are traces of Iranian customs, too, and from time to time they may have had Iranian rulers.

It is also logical to suppose that they followed the great rivers. In ancient times and indeed almost up to the present, the rivers were the only easy roads through the endless sea of grass (as these wide plains of south Russia were then called), and then through the tangled oak scrub north of them, and finally through the taiga, or pine-cone forest.

The rivers have always meant much to this people.

"Let us mount, brothers, upon our swift steeds, and look upon the blue Don!" cried one of their descendants. "I wish to bend and from my helmet drink of it!"

Even today some of their soul is expressed by the famous Volga boat song.

I cannot tell you, either, how much time their long migration took, but certainly it must have taken many centuries.

For by the time they arrived in Europe they were no longer a truly nomad people, if, indeed, they had ever been.

They lived in a place—or in several places, for they already numbered too many to be a single unit—made it their home; cut down or girdled the trees; built themselves shelters; penned in their livestock; and planted their crops. There they stayed for a while.

Then, either because they had used up the land's resources or because they were again under pressure from their enemies, they would move on again.

After that they would halt for a second time, and then once more continue to plod. Their movement was as imperceptible, but also as hard to stop and as inexorable, as the creeping shoreward of an incoming tide. But finally they came to four almost insurmountable obstacles.

To the west of them they found the Vistula River. This was as large and swollen as any they had left behind them, and beyond it were the warlike Germans.

In front of them was a long, shallow lagoon; then white sand dunes; and then a pallid body of water.

"*More!*" they shouted. "*More!* The sea! The sea!"

Later they would call it Baltiskoye More, or Sea of Whiteness.

But notice that their word *more*—it is similar to Latin *mare* and English *mere*—was closer to "marsh" or "moor" than it is to any word that means open ocean. It is because of this and of other words which we can study that we know that these wanderers and others of the red-brown group were originally an inland people.

To the northeast were the Pripet Marshes. These were a conglomeration of bogs, swamps, shallow lakes, and even rivers covering an area of thirty-five thousand square miles. In winter these Pripet Marshes freeze solid, but during the rest of the year they are a huge lake and are impassable.

To the south, in the distance, was a further obstacle: the jagged, high Carpathian Mountains.

Here our red-brown people halted. It was either difficult or impossible to go farther, and anyway the lands were almost empty. So it was in the large four-sided block of land between these barriers and between the upper reaches of the Dnieper, the Bug, and the Dniester rivers that they finally settled down.

If you look at a map, you will see that this area lies almost entirely in what today is eastern Poland and western Russia.

The Slavs, therefore—for these people were the ones we call the proto-Slavs or Slavic ancestors—had their first permanent home in what is still the heart of Slavdom. There they developed their first Slav qualities. You could almost say that they *became* Slavs there; that is, it was there that they made themselves different from the other sons of Japheth who were the Thracians, the Illyrians, the Hellenes, the Teutons, the Celts, the Italic people, and all the rest. They lived where there are still more Slavs—and Slavs who are more unmixed culturally and even racially—than anywhere else in the whole world.

Che field men
And the forest men

The early Slavs lived in a rude and backward fashion. Their descendants have become a complex group who have made almost every kind of contribution to almost all forms of civilization and culture. But when the Slavs first appeared, and for a long time afterward, they were very nearly the most primitive of the Indo-Europeans. Indeed, if you would like to know how the ancient Indo-Europeans probably lived, you need only to study the ancient Slavs.

They were kept this way by their distance from other peoples and their isolation.

Civilization—at any rate, our western civilization—seems to have started in fertile river valleys like the palm-bordered Nile and the slowly winding Tigris and Euphrates in what is now Iraq. From there it pushed outward to the seafaring people who carried it wherever their ships could go. The barbarians became civilized by coming into contact with those who already were. But except for an occasional Roman trader (Roman coins and Roman trinkets have been found by the

shores of the Baltic), hardly a person from any of the southern and by then civilized countries ever came into contact with these ancient Slavs.

Instead, they had for neighbors their close cousins the Balts, who were about the only Indo-Europeans who were less advanced than they. The Balts were the ancestors of the modern Lithuanians and Latvians and of the Borussians, or Old Prussians. To the west, they had the most isolated and least tamed of the Germans. To the south, they had those of the Iranians who were still nomads, and the northernmost and wildest of the wild Thracians. To the northeast of them, they had the

Finns and the Lapps. The Finns and Lapps—the latter with their famous reindeer—still lived in the Stone Age.

"*Me slafne prosta tschade,*" wrote a Slav prince to a Byzantine emperor. "We Slavs are a very simple people!" This was in the ninth century A.D., long after they had come into contact with other people.

If it was true then, it was certainly true in pagan times.

Lost in their marshes and wilderness, hidden in the dense miles of tall trees which began at the Danube and the Rhine and did not yield to the ax until the time of Charlemagne, they remained what they had always been. They remained the field men and the forest men: the farmer and the dweller in the wilderness.

As they migrated northward, they had grown wheat, barley, millet, rye, and oats. They had planted peas, beans, lentils, beets, onions, and garlic. They seem to have known about apples, pears, cherries, and plums.

They had kept geese, ducks, chickens, and perhaps pigeons. They had also bred cattle, and they had huge herds of sheep and swine.

One of the reasons the early Polish people had two names is that some of them—the husbandmen and cultivators—lived in the *polje,* or "fields," and became known as Polians, or field-dwellers. The name Pole comes from this. Others, the cattle breeders and the shepherds, lived in the *lyata,* or "meadows," and became known as Lyakhs. But they also lived off the wild woodlands and the teeming rivers and streams.

Into the labyrinth of swamps, they poled their double-ended craft, and there they netted or speared the pink-fleshed salmon. The trout. The pike. The sturgeon. And, of course, many others.

They hunted the aurochs, the Europeon bison, which was huge of size and black in color, and the buffalo with its long horns, fiery temper, and keen scent. These they took by digging pits and covering them with withes and branches. With their metal-tipped arrows and lances (at first bronze, but even before the Christian era, iron) they hunted and shot the red deer, the tall and mighty elk (whose antlers sometimes had an eleven-foot spread), the wild boar, and possibly the wild horse. Concealed in the brown sedges, they waited for the white swan and the wild goose and the wild duck to come whistling in. These they shot too.

They were also fur trappers. They trapped large animals like the hungry, marauding gray wolf and the shaggy brown bear. But they trapped marten, too, and sable and ermine and fox and otter and beaver and squirrel. The Slavs have always been, and some of them still are, the world's greatest trappers of small animals with valuable pelts. (The Greek and Roman words, as well as the English word for sable, are said to have come from the Slavs.)

The Slavs likewise robbed the bees of honey and of honeycomb.

They also cut wood in their deep and fragrant forests. Indeed, it was from trees toppled in the Russian forests that the fleet which attacked Constantinople had been built.

"The Krivichians," said Constantine Born-in-the-Purple, the Byzantine emperor, "and others in Slavland, cut the timbers and built their single-straked ships in winter, and when the ice melts they bring them to the neighboring lakes and thence float them to the Dniester."

This lumber, and the hulls made from it, and the beeswax and the honey, together with sable and mink and also salt fish and slaves, they sometimes used themselves, but more often they sold. It was the beeswax and the fur which probably brought more traders to the ancient Slav countries than anything else.

In return, they received fibulae (pins closely resembling safety pins), rings, heavy collars, and gold bracelets. There was very little gold mined in ancient Slavland, and its glint caught the chieftains' eyes.

The social customs of the pre-Christian Slavs were backward too.

Of course, we cannot believe everything we are told about

them. Much of our information comes either from the old German chronicles or from the Byzantines, and neither the Germans nor the Byzantines ever thought too highly of the Slavs. Yet we do know a few things about the pagan Slavs which show that they were still close to our savage ancestors.

Surplus population is always a problem to a backward people, for they hardly ever produce more than just enough food for their own needs in a good year, and in a bad year they face starvation.

Some of the ancient Slavs—the Baltic Slavs, the Pomeranians, the Lusatian Slavs, and others—took care of their surplus population by suffocating or drowning their unwanted infants. A mother would even drown her own unwanted daughter. In such a rude society, nobody seemed to think that there was anything wrong with this.

The pagan Slavs also killed old people when they could no longer work. This, of course, was also done by other primitive people. Only among the Slavs the custom lasted longer. As late as 1328, a German duke had to forbid the practice to an East Slav tribe which he had conquered. It is said that the practice lasted even longer than that in medieval Serbia.

The pagan Slavs also practiced polygamy right up to the day they embraced Christianity. That is, if they even had marriage at all in the sense which we understand it today.

The first Russian ruler to make his people Christian was Prince Vladimir of Kiev. He was a wicked old scoundrel, but be became Saint Vladimir.

In his pagan days, Prince Vladimir had five recognized wives and a harem of eight hundred ladies besides.

But he was no exceptional case. There was a Pomeranian prince who had twenty-four wives, and Duke Mieszko of Poland had at least seven. Just as Prince Vladimir was the first Russian ruler to make his people Christian, Duke Mieszko was the first Polish one. Indeed, it was he who put Poland under the Pope's authority and thus made her Roman Catholic. The Poles have been Roman Catholic ever since, although a majority of the other Slavic people became Eastern Orthodox.

These wives, incidentally, were not wooed and won by being courted in romantic fashion.

In the early days, when a Slav chieftain—or for that matter almost any young Slav—wanted a bride, he gathered together his followers or his friends, armed them, and descended on a neighboring clan or tribe. If they were lucky, and if their swords were sharp and well used, they came back with the loveliest young ladies in that clan. It is said that the young ladies did not object too much.

But once again this was not a unique Slavic custom. (Almost everybody remembers the story of the Sabine women!) But with the pagan Slavs this was a general practice, not just an isolated instance. Traces of it still linger in certain Slav countries, particularly Russia and the Balkans.

Louis Adamic returned to his own country in 1932, and there served as groomsman at his cousin's wedding. The bride-to-be came from another town, and as the groom's party conducted her to the church, they found a barrier of twisted willow shoots and field flowers across the road. Nobody was going to carry off one of their women!

This led to pretended use of force and finally to bargaining, some of which was very comic. For instance, was the bride-to-be really beautiful enough to bother about? Was a woman worth as much as an ox?

In the end an agreement was reached, and the young men

of the bride's village accepted a purchase price of five hundred dinars (in those days about seven dollars). They spent it at the nearest inn.

This too was in accordance with tradition, for purchase of one's bride was another old Slav custom. In fact, both practices were used among the early Slavs.

"Each Slavic tribe," reported the monk Sylvester, "had its own traditions and its own customs. The Polyanians"—these were the ones who settled in Kiev—"kept to the mild and peaceful ways of their forebears and showed respect to their mothers and fathers, and even their mothers-in-law and their brothers-in-law. They marry in this way. The groom's brother does not fetch the bride, but she is brought to the bridegroom in the evening, and in the morning they turn over the dowry." But only after long negotiations between the father of the bride and an older man representing the groom!

The Derevlians, on the other hand—these were the forest men; *dyerevo* still means "forest" in Russian—"lived like wild beasts. They killed one another and ate every kind of filth.

"There were no marriages among them, but only festivals, and when the people gathered together for dancing and for sport, the men took away the women they wanted. Sometimes they carried off two or three."

Or they made off with young girls when they went to the river to get water.

Whether she had been abducted or purchased, from then on the Slav maiden who became a Slav wife had a hard and difficult life. The widow of a prominent man was sometimes made the leader of a tribe or clan, and Slav women, especially if they lived to be very old, were often regarded as having ac-

quired much lore and wisdom and were treated with the respect due a healer or a prophetess. They were supposed to
know all the proverbs. Proverbs are very important to the
Slavs, who regard them as storehouses of accumulated knowl-
edge. But with these exceptions, the Slavic woman had few
rights and was supposed only to discharge household duties
and bring up the children.

With a son, even child rearing only lasted until he was seven
years old. At that age, or sometimes even younger, a few locks
were symbolically shorn from his head. This meant that he had
now become a man and was under his father's jurisdiction,
not his mother's. This ceremony was called *postrigy,* or
postrizhiny, and lasted into Christian times.

After a hard life, the primitive Slav usually had a barbaric
funeral, especially if he had been an important person. This
was called a *tyrza,* and was usually followed by a *strava,* or
wild feast where food and drink were plentiful. The corpse
was carried—or sometimes, even in summer, dragged on a
sled—to the pyre. If it was to be buried—the ancient Slavs
practiced both burial and cremation—it was taken to its
special tomb. It was clad and armed as in life and was
followed by men chanting the deceased's praise and by women
weeping and lamenting, tearing their faces with their finger-
nails, and even bruising their bodies and cutting off their hair.
As is still done in parts of the Balkans, they had all left the
house through a special opening. The regular doors and windows had been tightly closed to keep the soul from finding its
way back.

The fire was lit by relatives.

Then very frequently came a final rite: the voluntary death

or murder of the widow and, sometimes, servants. These victims were often plied with strong drink so that they would not realize what they were doing. When a young man died, sometimes a girl allowed herself to be slain so that he would have a companion in the world to come. Horses and dogs, of course, were often sacrificed.

But this act of self-sacrifice was practiced by many other ancient Indo-Europeans. The suttee of India, where a widow flung herself on her husband's pyre, was the most famous example. It was not legally abolished until 1829!

Yet we must not come to the conclusion that the ancient Slavic people had made no advances at all, or that they still lived as did the Stone Age people who had dwelt in Europe before their coming. This was very far from the case.

Just take the matter of food alone. The people who lived in Europe before the Indo-Europeans came certainly knew fire, and they undoubtedly roasted or grilled the game they caught. The Slavs did this too, but like the other Indo-Europeans they had progressed a great deal farther. Since they were cattle raisers, they ate beef from their own lowing herds and although some of the animals were scrawny and lean, their meat was juicy and tender. As swineherds they ate pork and bacon. As sheep raisers, they ate lamb and mutton. There is some reason to believe that they also ate pheasant or a game bird like pheasant, as well as chicken and other domestic fowl.

It goes without saying that they ate of the varied selection of vegetables they grew, no longer relying on wild berries and wild fruit.

But they drank fresh milk, too, and curdled milk and made cheese. There were words for all of these in the ancient Slavic tongues. Soon the Slavs were no longer eating their grain in the form of a moistened and then grilled mush, but were grinding flour on circular stone millstones and making bread or cakes.

Slav nut cakes and honey cakes were known and praised by the very earliest travelers. They are still praised today.

On the purely luxury side, the Slavs knew about and ate caviar even in pagan days. It is not certain that they considered it especially valuable, but everybody else has ever since.

The Slavs likewise made more than one intoxicating beverage. They did not use wine until somewhat later, for the vine did not grow naturally in their ancient homeland. But they made hydromel and mead by fermenting water and honey— one of their ancient chieftains had one hundred barrels of mead as his principal treasure—and as far back as is known, they brewed and drank beer. They brewed it out of barley or oats. Hops were not introduced until much later.

Drinking was very important to the early Slavs. It was so important that their word for banquet (*piru*) came from *piti*, which means "to drink." Even the Slav women were often heavy drinkers.

"She drinks and she rides like a warrior," said the German chronicler Thietmar of a medieval Slavic princess.

Feasting was important to the Slavs too, and here also they had progressed very far beyond their Stone Age predecessors.

"In the olden times," wrote the Byzantine emperor Leo the Philosopher, "the Slavs were very zealous in their practice of hospitality. Even today, not to be hospitable to strangers is regarded as a sin."

That was written in 900. It was still true one thousand years later. I myself once took a carriage for more than sixty miles across the mountains of central Yugoslavia, and then a train to Sarajevo where World War I was started. The trip lasted a whole day, and during that time my traveling companions would not let me pay for so much as a single cup of coffee. I was a stranger visiting their country!

During their pagan days, this hospitality took the form of their always being able to entertain any visitor lavishly.

"Their table is never bare," said a traveler. "It is always spread and every head of a family makes sure that he has all the food and drink that is needful. You can be served at any hour."

Sometimes as many as twenty dishes were offered. The tables were usually round, and it was the custom to sit on the floor. There were no forks, and even wooden spoons were rare. But every feaster had a knife. Although a prince might be surrounded by forty favorites, there were no social distinctions until Christianity came. Then those who had not been baptized had to sit at the door!

The Slavs also developed their own clothing and were very proud of it. When the Slavs first began to come into contact with other Europeans, King Dagobert of France—he is the one they have a nursery rhyme about—sent an ambassador to King Samo of Bohemia. But King Samo would not receive him.

"Not until he puts on the costume of my people," he decreed.

Even as late as 1124, a German bishop visiting some pagan Slavs decided he would make many more converts if he put on native garb.

This costume was a great improvement on the rawhide-stitched bearskins and deerskins of the Stone Age people. It was very different from them, but it was also different from the chitons and togas of the Greeks and Romans. The latter were designed for olive groves or sun-drenched forums. The Slavic costume was designed to keep the wearer warm.

For the men it consisted of a coarse shirt made of dirty gray linen or hemp (the Slavs did not know how to bleach) which fell to the knees. Legs were pushed into long tight trousers, tied in at the ankles or thrust into woolen stockings, and held up by a belt of rope or leather. Sometimes, instead of the shirt the ancient Slavs wore a short tunic like the modern Russian *rubashka.* In cold weather, they wore over it a long coat trimmed or even lined with fur. But the poorer Slavs wore coats of sheepskin. In the Balkans, they do today.

The Slav women were clad in a long skirt or wrapper, also of linen or hemp. It was a mere cylinder of fabric held up by straps over the shoulders. Maybe it was the ancestor of the modern sheath!

Footwear consisted of bits of leather with slightly upturned edges and was held in place by a strap or by a band wound about the calf. Slippers made of bast, or woven fiber, were also worn. The men wore high felt hats, sometimes with a narrow brim, but often they wore conical hats of fur. Married women had their hair cropped, and it was kept covered. Maidens went bareheaded and had long and flaxen braids. Most of the men wore their hair long and brushed away from their fore-heads. Almost all of them had beards.

Last of all—and almost from their first days in Europe—the Slavs lived in weatherproof houses grouped into towns and villages.

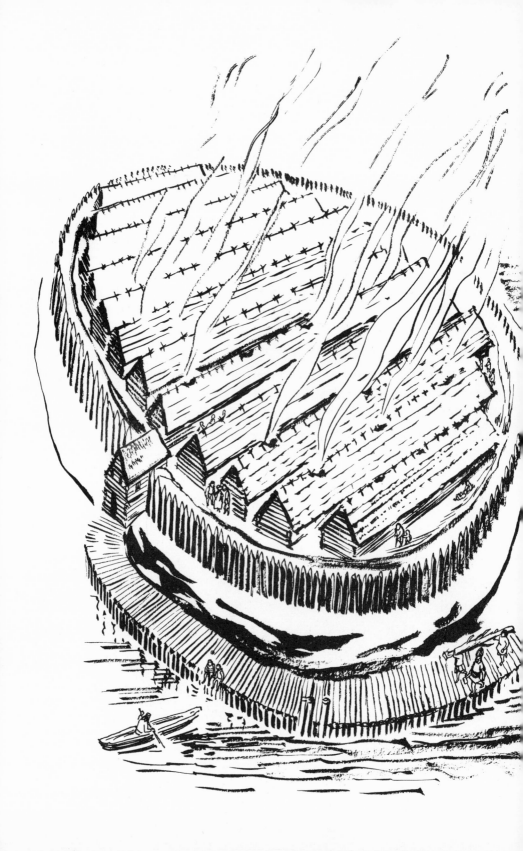

One of the common Slav words is *gorod* or *grad,* which we see even today in city names like Beo*grad* (Belgrade), Petro*grad,* Nishni-Nov*gorod.* (The Slavs also spoke of Constantinople as Tsar*grad.*) It is almost the same as garden and it meant "enclosed place." Later it came to mean "city" or "town."

The ancient Slavs lived in these *grads.* Indeed, the vikings often called Russia Garderyk, or Town Kingdom.

"Four thousand, six hundred of them," wrote the famous English historian Edward Gibbon, "were scattered over the provinces of Russia and Poland, and their huts were hastily built of rough timber. We may compare them to the architecture of the beaver!"

Actually, they were a great deal better than that. An Arab geographer said that in the olden days the Slavs lived in under-

ground cellars which were little more than three-foot-deep ditches with a rude covering. That may have been true in the beginning, but soon most Slavs were constructing log cabins not too different from those built by pioneers in the United States.

A typical Slav cabin consisted of a single room. The walls were made of tree trunks; the roof was covered with reeds or thatched. In the center was a hearth and above this a hole to let out smoke. Chimneys were a much later development. Around the walls were low benches of claylike earth which served as seats or beds. (Everybody—men, women, and children—slept in this room, everybody ate there, and sometimes even the animals found shelter there.) It was not until nearly the end of pagan days that there were any improvements. Then a vestibule was added, the floor became wooden instead of earth, and an oven replaced the open hearth.

But even in these earliest days, there was often a typical Slav adjunct, although some think that the idea came from the Sarmatians who lived on the steppes.

One of the oldest Slav legends is that Saint Andrew, the brother of Saint Peter, visited Poland and Russia in the first days of the Christian era.

"I saw the Slav lands," he reported, "and while I was among them, I noticed their wooden bathhouses. They warm them to extreme heat, then undress, and after anointing themselves with an acid liquid, they take young branches and lash their bodies. They do this so violently that sometimes they barely escape alive. Then they drench themselves with cold water and are revived."

In point of fact, this is probably a made-up story. It is unlikely that Saint Andrew visited any Slavic people. But what he is supposed to have related about them is absolutely true.

The ancient Slavs actually did build wooden bathhouses near their huts and cabins. They actually did lash themselves with besoms. They actually did revive themselves with icy water, or by leaping into snowbanks.

The pagan Slavs also made and used soap, and that long before any perfumed soap was brought to them by the early traders.

Indeed, in spite of all the things said about their unclean habits by the first historians, so important were these heated baths to them that the Russian word for "cottage" or "small house" is derived from an earlier word meaning "steam room" or "stove."

GOVERNMENT AND GODS

In these villages—sometimes they were circular in shape, but other *gorods* or *grads* were rectangular with parallel streets—in these little towns set at the edge of a morass, or on a tree-crowned hilltop above the whirlpools and eddies where two rivers met, or even in the dim and dusky aisles between ancient oak trees or lofty pines, the first Slavs organized whatever civic or community life they had. Here they worked out their first, primitive form of government.

It was a combination of a very simple farmer collectivism (ownership by the group) with a patriarchal, or old man, rule.

The fundamental basic unit was the family, or at most a group of families who were very closely related. Among the ancient Poles this was called the *rod,* or "kinfolk," but in other Slavic places it had other names. In Croatia and some other South Slav lands, there were similar organizations called *zadrugas,* while in the mountains of old Serbia and Montenegro there was a unit known as the *kuća. Kuća* means "house" or "home." There were *zadrugas* and *kućas* in these areas right up to World War II. Their members were often far more loyal to them than they were to the state or the nation.

You would kill—and many did—to avenge a wrong done to one of those belonging to the same *kuća*. Even in modern times some of the feuds lasted for generations.

This is how a *rod* was made up. There was a white-haired father or grandfather. There was his wife, white-haired too, her face lined with the cares of generations. There were his younger brothers with their wives. There were his sons with their wives; his unmarried daughters; his brothers' sons with their wives; his brothers' unmarried daughters; and a tumbling array of grandnieces and grandnephews. But no married daughters or married nieces. They had moved away to join the *rods* of their husbands. All in all, there were hardly ever less than forty or fifty persons in a *rod*, and some numbered as many as one hundred.

The grandfather—or if he died, his oldest remaining brother, or at any rate the oldest male—was the ruler of this *rod*. (Theoretically there was an election. The *rod* met to choose a new ruler, but the oldest male was almost always named.) He was known as the *starosta* or *starešina*. *Staraj* or *star* (or a word that sounds much the same) means "old" in almost every Slavic language. But we use the same idea in the English words "elder" or "alderman," and the Romans used it in *senator*, which comes from *senex*, meaning "old" too.

This *starosta* had almost absolute powers.

"You will be the ox man," he said. "You the sheep man. You the lamb man. You the pig man. You the barnyard fowl man. You the barley man!"

He also decided who would plow which fields and what would be planted in them. He had to. For the early Slavs owned everything in common. It was not until they came into contact with the Germans and others that they even began to have an idea of private property.

Instead, as they moved northward into the empty miles of their new home, they first took possession of the land, for land was what they wanted most of all.

Then they settled it.

Finally, they left it to their heirs.

But no man left it to his sons and to his grandsons, for the forests and the fields could not be divided. For that matter, not even the hooked sickles, the colters and the spades, the primitive plows, could be divided either. They were too important to the *rod's* survival, so all of them were left to the group. In the beginning, the plows were extremely simple, hardly more than a pointed stick attached to a wooden shaft, but later they resembled modern plows. At first, they were pulled by dogs or even by the plowman himself, but before long, oxen and horses were used.

The *starosta* was also the military leader. The primitive Slavs were an agricultural people, and agricultural people do not usually have a taste for wars of conquest. The season for fighting is summer, and that is also the season for growing things. Why sacrifice the second for the first?

But they did have to defend themselves, for they were surrounded by people who thought that crops others had grown and harvested made excellent booty.

For that reason, virtually every Slav village was organized to protect itself. It had a wall of earth—in front of this was a ditch—or a fence or a stockade of wooden palings. There was also usually a wooden watchtower. These watchtowers, in fact, the town itself, could be set on fire. There is a story of how the Russian princess Olga once captured a Derevlian Slav stronghold by attaching firebrands to sparrows they had given her as tribute, and then releasing them. They flew back to their nests in the eaves, and the place was burned down. But the towers were strong enough to withstand the rocks hurled by the rudimentary stone throwers of their enemies, and the walls were strong too. They were a refuge in times of danger.

The Slavs were also skillful at the kind of guerrilla warfare that was practiced by the American Indians. It is said, for example, that when they were hard pressed they would retreat to a marshy lake and lie hidden under its waters all day while breathing through the long tube of a hollow reed. Then when the enemy withdrew, they would come out and harass them. They had no cavalry. They did not need any. But equipped lightly, they could slip through the trees unseen and then come out to surprise and often defeat the foe.

It was up to the *starosta* to decide whether his people should do this or retreat to the villages and towns.

The *starosta* was also judge and to some extent jury.

Primitive Slav justice was swift and also ruthless. The right to retaliate was recognized. It was an eye for an eye and a tooth for a tooth if the offended party wanted it. Moreover, there was no long waiting. A criminal taken in the act could be, and usually was, punished then and there.

But the whole *rod* was responsible for anything a member did, and if the offense was against a second *rod*, the first *rod* had to see that reparations were made.

Must the wrongdoer be executed, or would an indemnity paid in silver be sufficient? This too was up to the *starosta*.

It was not until well toward the end of the pagan era that groups of families united to make tribes or clans. After that, of course, it was hard for the *starosta* to exercise his old authority. For there was now no definitely established head of a single unit. The chieftain either had to seize power or be elected to power. Besides that there was now a *wiece,* or council, to complicate matters.

It was probably the conduct of this council that earned the Slavs their reputation for wrangling democracy. The council met in a special building in the center of the *grad,* and every free adult male could take part in its deliberations. Most of them did. Since every Slav now felt himself the equal of every other Slav, the sessions were usually stormy.

It was not until nearly Christian times—and then under direct foreign influence or under foreign pressure or even conquest—that the Slavic tribes took the final step and united to become Slavic nations.

The very word *knez,* or *kniaz,* meaning "prince" is a corruption of the Old High German *kuning,* which meant "king." The word *korol,* or *kralj,* which means "king," is a corruption of Karl. Karl was Charlemagne. In spite of their contacts with the Byzantines, Charlemagne seemed to the Slavs the greatest king that they had ever known. So if you were crowned in a Slavic country, you were the *Karl* of Poland or the *Karl* of Bohemia or the *Karl* of Serbia.

But, of course, even Tsar, or for that matter Kaiser, is a corruption of Caesar.

By that time the Slavs had long since abandoned their simple family social structure. There were now three clearly divided classes in most of Slavland.

At the bottom of the ladder were the slaves, and many people think that the English word "slave" comes from *Slav*. Many captives in Southeast Europe were of Slavic origin, and soon all captives became known as "Slavs" and then in English "slaves." These slaves were either remnants of the native people whom the Slavs found when they moved into new lands, prisoners of war, or Slavs who had sold themselves or their children to pay off their debts. They were not treated badly. Their masters called them their children. Even if they were prisoners of war, they could redeem themselves. But they had no rights.

Next came the freemen. These were the descendants of the old members of the *rod*, the hard-working field men and forest men who are still at the back of almost every solid Slav achievement.

Finally, there was a smaller class of fighting and later land-owning nobles, some of whom were not even Slav by race. They were called the *szlachta*, or *schlehta*, in Poland and Bohemia, but they were the boyars of Russia or Bulgaria.

You have already seen the boyars in action. They made up the prince's personal following, like the *druzhina* of sword-brandishing Northmen and Slavs who marched with Askold and Dir!

The Slavs also developed their own religion in these early days.

As soon as man began to think, he began to wonder who had made him and what powers ruled the world in which he lived. The Slavs were no exception. Silently herding their swine, their goats, their sheep, drifting down the yellow Niemen or yellow Vistula, plowing their stubborn fields or penetrating the woodland and the wold, they wondered why they were lashed by drenching rains or kept homebound by the deep and silent snow. They wondered why the lightning darted out of heaven like a crisp blue snake and why white-crested storm waves lashed the white Baltic dunes. They wondered why they were first frozen to death and then scorched by intolerable heat, why rivers overflowed into hard-worked fields; why crops were spoiled by mildew or rats, or livestock perished; and yet sometimes the spring winds were gentle and kind, and the heavens above billowed with a foam of clouds or were frosted with stars at night.

The Slavs found an answer in a series of deities and spirits that were more like forces of nature than the concept of God as we understand it. Indeed, their very name for God—Bog— was not the *deus* or Zeus of the Romans and Greeks but came from an old Iranian word *bag,* or *baga,* which meant "wealthy" or "plenty."

Under the wide vault, they worshiped Svarog, the Sky, with his sons Dazhbog, the Sun, and Svarogich, Fire. They also sometimes worshiped the Sun's bald old uncle Myesyats, the Moon.

Plowing the black soil, they worshiped Mati Syra Zemlya, Mother Moist Earth.

"Mother Moist Earth," they said, "smite every wicked and unclean being so that he may not cast any spell on us or bring us any evil."

Then their days would be good, and all that they had sown would prosper.

They also had a whole host of minor deities. There was the household spirit (*domovoi*); the spirit of the bath (*bannik*);

the barn or shed spirit (*ovinnik*); the field spirit (*polevik*); the woodland spirit (*leshky*); the various water spirits; and many others.

Most of these spirits were either gnomelike in appearance or wizened old men and old women. They survive even today as demons, goblins, and wicked stepmothers.

But at least one of the water spirits was beautiful and charming. She was the *rusalka* of Russia or the *vila* of the Danube Serbs. Both were the souls of drowned maidens, but they had very different characters. The *rusalka* was cruel and tried to lure men and women into drowning too, but the *vila* was kind and did many favors. There are still supposed to be *vilas* in Yugoslavia, and even as recently as the beginning of this century, a learned scholar wrote that he had heard one singing. But you can make up your mind for yourself.

Most of these gods and goddesses were not worshiped formally. They had neither altar nor temple, although some of them were adored under a towering oak which thus got a sacred character. Unlike the Celts with their hoary druids, very few of the Slavs had a priestly class. The *starosta* in the early days and the prince later, were the only high priests they had.

The Baltic Slavs were almost the only exception.

Saxo Grammaticus, the medieval Danish historian who first gave us the story of Hamlet, tells about the island of Rügen off the coast of Germany in the Baltic Sea. At Arkona on this island, the Slavic people had constructed a magnificent temple to Svantovit, their war god. It was a huge place with ornately carved pillars, and in its center was a statue of the god himself. He was four-headed (or really four-faced), and each face looked in a different direction. He had two hands for each

face, and in one of these hands was a bull's horn filled with pre-
cious liquor. At his side was a mighty sword and near-by was
a huge saddle and an enormous bridle. Saddled close at hand,
and carefully groomed, was a splendid white horse.

The bull's horn and the white horse played important parts
in the ritual. Once a year on a fixed and stated day, a long-

Perun

Svantovit

robed and ancient high priest examined the bull's horn. If it was still filled, the year would be a good one. At the same time the white horse was driven through a complicated pattern of spears. He went through at a gallop and if he caught none of them with his hoofs, that was a good sign too.

Perun—we have already heard the followers of Askold and Dir shouting his name—was another god who was worshiped formally, although unlike Svantovit, he did not have a special class of priests. He was the thunder god, but he was also the war god. This did not seem inconsistent to the pagan Slavs, for the thunderbolt was supposed to be a divine weapon.

There was a statue of Perun at Kiev even more magnificent than the one of Svantovit at Arkona. It towered high into the air, and if it was carved out of a mighty tree, it had a head of silver and mustaches of gold. In its hand was a golden lance which represented lightning. (But some Slavs said that Perun carried instead a millstone which he rolled above the heavens.) It flashed in the sunlight as its worshipers bowed to it.

Perun—and Svantovit and Volos and Triglav and Trojanu and many other gods, as well as all the water nymphs and household deities—were worshiped for a much longer time than were any other pagan gods in Europe.

For although Christianity was not officially recognized by the Roman state until Constantine I (306–337) became a Christian, the new faith was widespread along the shores of the Mediterranean within one hundred years of the Crucifixion. France, western Germany, England, and even Ireland had accepted Christianity before the year 500.

But no Slavic people became Christian until 870. (The Bulgarians and the Bohemians were about the first.) The Russians did not become Christians until almost 1000. Some of the Pomeranians—and then only because of the fire and sword of the invading Teutonic Knights—were not converted until 1250.

Finally, Duke Jagello of Lithuania was not baptized until

1386. To be sure, he was a Lithuanian not a Slav, but he had many Slav subjects who did not become Christians until he did.

So there were Slavs worshiping pagan gods as recently as one hundred years before Columbus discovered America. Possibly some Slavs worshiped them even longer!

This is an important thing to remember. It is important to remember that there is something deep in the Slavic character that makes them want to cling to the old.

Even now the Slavic languages are nearer to the language spoken by the first Indo-Europeans than is any other language, and each Slav language is more like every other Slav language than is true of Germanic languages like German and English, or Romance languages like Italian or French. Slavs hold on to their language, even when they are conquered and oppressed, as no other people do.

Their old ways of living together have lasted longer and have had more effect on their modern institutions.

But when they were finally exposed to new influences, they accepted these eagerly, and did not very often look backward.

But that could not happen until they had emerged from the forests and fens in which they had dwelt for at least two thousand years.

PEOPLE ON ThE MARCh

Around the year 200 A.D. something began to happen in the borderlands of Europe and beyond them throughout almost all of Asia north of the Himalaya Mountains.

There began a moving and a migration of the nations.

Historians call this the *Völkerwanderung,* or "folk wandering." But they don't all agree on what brought it about.

When I was a student, for example, I was taught that it was the Great Wall of China. This wall, which is 1,500 miles long and 25 feet high, was completed around 204 B.C. Supposedly it kept the Hsiung Nu, and other northern barbarians from pushing southward into China, and so they rode westward instead. The western barbarians fled before them.

But others say it was a change of climate: central Asia became arid instead of fertile.

But whatever the reason was, there was no place from Jutland on the North Sea to Lake Baikal far away on the very borders of Mongolia where people did not seethe and stir.

The Teutonic people—the Vandals, the Visigoths, the Ostrogoths, the Franks, the Angles, the Saxons, and many, many others—left their homes beyond the Rhine to move into

64

places as far apart and as different as France, Italy, England, Spain, and North Africa. It was this spreading out that brought about the downfall of the mighty Roman Empire. At almost the same time, Turkic and the Turko-Tatar people like the Avars, the Khazars, and the terrible Huns, folded their felt tents near the Altai Mountains on the borders of distant Mongolia, and mounted their little Tatar ponies to begin a long trek which took them past Lake Balkhash, Lake Aral, and the Caspian Sea to southern Russia and in some cases to the heart of Europe. But even in Arabia—although this is not usually considered part of the *Völkerwanderung*—the desert nomads began to explode outward from their stony peninsula. By the eighth century, they had reached Persia in one direction and Spain or southern France in the other.

At almost the same time and probably for the same reason or reasons, the Slavic peoples began to seethe and stir. In their distant corner of Europe, they too began to migrate and move.

They moved in almost every direction.

If you look at a map illustrating their early history, you will see a shaded area representing the original Slav home, and from it arrows radiate to all points of the compass.

One arrow points to the west. The march of the Teutons had left much of Germany without population, and sometime probably before 500 A.D. their neighbors to the east moved in to fill the vacuum. The Polabian Slavs (*po*, "along," *Labe*, "the Elbe") settled on or near the lacy network of mud flats from which one day the great city of Hamburg would arise. It is even possible (in spite of the fact that its name comes from an old German word meaning "forest") that Hamburg was originally a Slav village. A little to the northeast, the

Pomeranians (*Pomorze*, from *po*, "along," *more*, "the sea") gave up livestock herding and even farming to become sea fighters and pirates. They were said to be the first people to devise ships to carry horses. We saw them worshiping Svantovit in an earlier chapter. The Lusatians and the Sorabians moved into what today are Brandenburg and Saxony.

(Incidentally, there are still a few Lusatians southeast of Berlin, and they are still Slavs. They were the only ones who were not driven out or absorbed by the returning Germans. They form a little Slavic island in the German sea.)

But other arrows point to the northeast, the east, the southeast, and the south; and these show the direction in which other Slavic people drifted or marched.

The Derevlians (the rude forest men), the Krivichians, the Polotians, and many others with equally difficult names moved to the northeast. There, as wolves howled and the evergreens were weighted down with snow, axes rang as the pioneers made clearings in the forest or even built forts or villages.

(One of these forts or villages became Novgorod, or New City. Novgorod was one of the most important Slav cities of the Middle Ages. It was so powerful that it called itself Lord Novgorod the Mighty. It traded with the Hanseatic towns of Germany and even with England, where bearded Novgorods walked the streets of London. By 1100, its sealers had penetrated the arctic as far as Novaya Zemlya which is less than one thousand miles from the North Pole.)

Others of the East Slav people—the Slavs now began to be divided into the East Slavs, the West Slavs, and the South Slavs as they are today—moved eastward or even southeastward instead of north or northeast. They moved slowly back toward the undulating green-gold, tall grass plains of their Indo-European ancestors. Here, the grass was so high that although they could see the blue and lilac of the cornflowers and hear the whistling of partridges, they could not see a man on horseback, or at best only his head.

These Slavic peoples were the Polyanians, the Duletians, the Volhynians, and various others which are listed by old Sylvester. Like their kinsmen to the north, they simply drifted. Theirs was not a military invasion like the invasion of Italy led by the Vandal Alaric or by Attila the Hun. As they had done from time immemorial, they simply tore down or abandoned their houses, picked up their farm implements, and gathered together their livestock. Their kinsmen to the north had sought taller trees and more plentiful fur-bearing animals. Their quest was for richer soil.

But the Slavic people who moved southward and southwestward were very different. They knew where they were going, and they had reason for going there. (The warmer climate, the riches, and the emptying lands of the Roman or the Byzantine empires.) Or if not, they were in the pay or under the command of people who did.

It would not be possible to name all of them. The Slavic tribes were still too numerous, and the historians of those olden days sometimes mixed up one with the other. But the White Serbians—these may have been some of the Sorabians of Germany—the White Croats, and the ancestral Czechs and Slovaks were among the most important.

Led by a legendary Servus, a legendary Prince Czech, and a legendary Chrovatos, or Chrobatos—these were probably

clan names attached to an imaginary first leader, but Chrovatos may have been an Iranian chieftain who taught the
ancient Slavs the first rudiments of military organization—
they climbed slowly up the gentle Sudeten Pass amid its ver-
dant hills, or even crossed the wilder and steeper Carpathian
Mountains.

They were now arrayed for battle.

They were still accustomed, as Procopius noted when he
first saw them, to hide behind small rocks or any bush which
might happen to be near, and they still fought on foot and
almost naked.

"Not only do they not wear body armor," said Procopius,
"but they do not even wear a shirt. And they gather up their
trews as far as they can."

But they now carried small shields and javelins, frequently
poisoned, and they were now very willing to engage in hand-
to-hand combat.

Behind them followed the women, the children, and even
the old. They carried all their household goods with them, for
they still did not use wagons.

The Czechs and the Slovaks halted by the Morava River
and in the mountains to the east and to the west of it. There
they mingled with their predecessors, Celtic and even pre-
Celtic, to become among the darker and more round-headed
of the Slavs.

But the other Slavic peoples, the Croats and the Serbs and
even the Slovenes, continued even farther. By the year 500
they had reached the Danube. Not much later—almost certainly as Avar mercenaries—they crossed it. Thus they reached
Salona (532), Durazzo (now called Dürres) in modern Albania

(548), and they spread out into Thrace, even reaching the walls of Constantinople.

These were the South Slavs (with the exception of the Czechs and Slovaks who were West Slavs). Other West Slavs—and the most important of these were the Lyakhs and the Mazovians and the other ancestors of the Poles—remained where they were. They alone live in the ancestral Slav home.

All this took place in historic times, but it also took place very early indeed. Certainly the Slav migrations were well under way by the fifth century, for in 484 A.D. there was a magnificent Slav funeral in the center of an Avar ring near present-day Vienna. That meant that there was a Slav prince there.

They had reached a high-water mark not more than two hundred or three hundred years later. By 700 A.D. or no later than 800 A.D.—which was when Charlemagne was crowned emperor and when Harun al-Rashid listened to *The Arabian Nights*—there were Slavic people in at least parts of every country which is Slavic today.

They have been there ever since.

The SLAVS IN The MIDDLE AGES

It was in these new places and in these new homes that they took the final step forward. It was at this time and in these lands that the Slavic clans and tribes began to unite into the Slavic nations as we know them now.

Today there are five predominantly Slavic states: Poland, Czechoslovakia, Yugoslavia, Bulgaria, and Soviet Russia.

(Of course, not every one of these is 100 per cent Slav, and there are Slavic enclaves in neighboring countries, but this mixture of peoples is something we must get used to when we study European history.)

Every single one of them was at least partly descended from an empire or a kingdom or a principality or a dukedom which existed in the Middle Ages.

Bohemia, which with its sister state, Moravia, was the forerunner of modern Czechoslovakia, was probably the first one to take shape and form. I have already mentioned King Samo, the one who told Dagobert's envoy he would have to wear Slavic clothing. Samo was a Frank (or possibly even a Celtic) merchant who defeated the Avars and built up the earliest Slavic kingdom of which we know. It occupied almost all of southern central Europe. Samo's reign began in 631 and lasted until 659.

But even if we do not count Samo as the creator of the Bohemian state—and maybe we shouldn't, since his empire collapsed at his death—we do have to count the legendary founder of the first Czech dynasty. He also lived very early indeed.

This is the story. The first known ruler of any Czech tribes was that same Prince Czech (although some say his name was Krok, or Krak) who had led his people across the mountains from their old ancestral home. This Czech had two sons and a granddaughter, Libuša, who was to go down in Czech folklore as not only the most beautiful, but the wisest princess who had ever lived.

For when Czech's sons quarreled over their father's inheritance, she too was summoned to appear before the council of chieftains which had been called together to settle the matter.

"You must either divide the inheritance and leave us weak," she told the bearded chieftains. "Or you must give it to one person."

"To one person!" they thundered.

Then, to her astonishment, they gave it not to either brother, but to Libuša.

"But I cannot rule alone," she said.

"Then choose a husband."

She did. She had heard of a wise and respected peasant whose name was Přemysl. To him she sent an emissary who found him seated at his cottage door.

"Princess Libuša wishes you to marry her and to share the rule of the land."

Přemysl put down the bread and cheese he had been munching.

"I will," he replied. "That is, if I can keep on wearing my peasant boots so people will know where I came from."

Přemysl and Libuša are still beloved, for they not only governed well, but they also told the people never to forget how to govern themselves.

"If you have too strong a ruler," said Libuša, "you can only say 'Yes, sire; yea, lord' to him. He will tell you where you must live and labor, and he will condemn you without trial."

I cannot help having a feeling that deep in their hearts many Czechs remember this still!

Among the many accomplishments of Přemysl and Libuša was the legendary founding of the city of Prague. The Czech name for Prague is Praha, and there are Slavic words *prah* and *prach* meaning "dust." Maybe once upon a time it was a dusty marketplace! Indeed, although archaeologists say that its site has been occupied since the Stone Age, that is what it still was then.

But under the influence of Libuša and Přemysl its wooden huts were replaced by sturdy edifices and by turreted walls. In due time, there was a castle and later two of them. The field men and the forest men were indeed becoming the city men. By 996, Prague could be described by an Arab traveler as "a city built of stone and lime, and one of the richest commercial centers of Europe." Today, of course, it is a modern industrial city with almost 1 million inhabitants.

Přemysl and Libuša were the first of a royal line which lasted until 1306. The two last Přemyslids are mentioned by Dante in his *Divine Comedy* although not in a very compli-

Slovaks

mentary manner. It was a Přemyslid who sent to Byzantium for Saint Cyril and Saint Methodius. These were the missionaries who converted much of Slavdom to Christianity.

(Saint Cyril has another claim to fame. It was he who developed the primitive Slav alphabet which later was modified and improved and named the Cyrillic alphabet. With a few variations from country to country, it is now used by the Russians, the Bulgarians, and the Serbians. It looks hard, but it is easy

once you learn it. The other Slavs use our own alphabet
although with special signs to indicate special sounds. Having
two alphabets is one of the things which in the olden days
helped keep the Slavs divided.)

The "good King Wenceslas" of the Christmas carol was a
Přemyslid too.

But even after the Přemyslid dynasty had ended, Bohemia
still flourished and had many famous kings. Perhaps the most
notable was Charles I, who became the German emperor
Charles IV. Then, for a while at least, the Czechs ruled
Germany instead of vice versa.

Charles was a Luxemburger by birth, but he was Czech in
all his feelings; he gave his sons Slavic names; he himself
spoke Czech and did everything he could to advance Czech
culture. Among his accomplishments, he founded the University
of Prague in 1348. It was the first university in central Europe.

But the great Czechs of the Middle Ages were not all mon-
archs. John Huss, who is generally considered one of the great
religious reformers of all time, did most of his teaching during the reign of Charles's incompetent successor, another
Wenceslas. Huss was burned at the stake, but his spirit went
marching on. One-eyed John Žižka was another great medieval Czech. He was a general on the Hussite side during the
civil wars that followed Huss's execution. He was the inventor
of modern tactics, the first one to use really mobile artillery—
the first artillery was usually very heavy and dragged by
oxen—and he was the first to use baggage wagons as mobile
cover. These Czechs were known and admired throughout all
Europe.

Poland had a legendary first ruler too. The first historical

John Huss   *John Žižka*

"duke of Poland" was that same Mieszko I who was the first Pole to be converted to Christianity. Mieszko married a Czech princess, thus uniting his own country with Bohemia, and although he did for a time have to acknowledge German suzerainty, he definitely established Polish rule not only in the ancient Polish lands but in new lands between the Oder and the Warthe rivers. That is, in the part of Germany which has again become Polish since World War II.

But actually he was the fifth ruler in his famous line. Its founder was Mieszko's great-great-grandfather, the semi-mythical Piast. Piast was said to have been a wheelwright by profession. He was a truly Homeric character.

In his youth, the Polish tribe to which he belonged was governed by a certain Popiel. Popiel was a surly character who had outraged Slav notions of hospitality by refusing to entertain two pilgrims. He was a pagan, and they were Christians!

It was at about this time that Piast was to celebrate the *postrizhiny,* the coming-to-manhood haircutting, of his oldest son. A banquet was in order, and annoyed at Popiel's stinginess, Piast decided to make it a good one. Maybe he was influenced too by the prophecy that his sons would rule all Poland.

Popiel came to this banquet as did almost every Polish chieftain. How could he feed them all?

Lo and behold, a miracle. A small flagon of hydromel overflowed every wine tun in Piast's home, and the flesh of a single hog filled barrel after barrel.

Then at the height of the eating and drinking which lasted several days, Popiel was found to be missing. A search was begun. He was found dead in a hogshead. The rats had half devoured him. Piast was chosen ruler in his stead.

Poles

Castle of Kraków

The line of Piast ruled for more than five hundred years. It produced many mighty rulers and some weak, ineffective ones. The most important was Casimir III, the last of the line, who reigned from 1333 to 1370. He is the only Polish monarch to be called "the Great."

Casimir was someone who today would be called a "liberal." He was known as "the Peasants' king" because he protected

Tomb of Casimir the Great

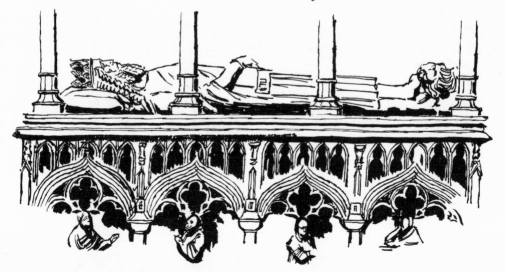

them and in time of famine, fed them. He built up national defense; promoted trade and industry; restricted the influence of the Germans who had flooded into the country as artisans and farmers; gave many privileges to the Jews; and not many years after Charles IV had founded the University of Prague, Casimir founded his own university at Kraków. This would soon be almost as renowned. (In fact, hardly 150 years later, it educated one of the world's most outstanding scientists, Copernicus—his real name in Polish was Mikolaj Kopernik— who discovered that the earth revolves about the sun.)

Casimir had no direct heirs, but he provided for the succession by leaving his throne to Louis the Great, King of Hungary. Louis, in turn, left it to his youngest daughter, Jadwiga.

Flaxen-haired Jadwiga is the heroine of a romantic story which changed the whole history of Poland. As a child she was brought up with Wilhelm of Hapsburg, a handsome young Austrian prince, and she was deeply in love with him. They would marry and live happily ever afterward!

But when the gay-hearted princess came to Kraków to be crowned "king" of Poland, the Polish noblemen told her that she would have to give up her girlhood lover and wed the wild Jagello, Duke of Lithuania, who was harrying their lands. After a long struggle between her heart and her duty, Jadwiga agreed. She made a good wife, and she so tamed Jagello—who became king of Poland when he married her—that when he died long after she did, he was seated on a balcony listening to her favorite nightingales.

It was under the Jagellons that medieval Poland reached its peak. Lithuania was three times its size, and together they

made up an empire that extended to the shores of the Black Sea and included most of western Russia. After the Battle of Tannenberg (1410) when the Poles and Lithuanians—aided by Bohemian mercenaries under our old friend John Žižka—crushed the dread Teutonic Knights, it reached to the Baltic too.

This also was the period in which Poland became an intellectual equal of western Europe. It was a Jagellon—Sigismund I—who married Bona Sforza whose uncle had been the patron of Leonardo da Vinci. When she arrived she brought Renaissance culture with her. Polish poets began to flourish, and one of them exchanged letters with the famous French poet Ronsard who regarded him as an equal. Cardinal Hosius be-

came one of the principal defenders of the Catholic Church. His works were read in Rome as well as in Warsaw. But most of all Renaissance architecture changed the face of Poland's cities. Tombs, chapels, and palaces—all in the best Italian style—spread over the country. Those on Wawel Hill in Kraków, where the Polish royal family had its residence, compared with many in Florence or Rome.

But shortly after that, there set in a decline. The last Jagellon died in 1572, and before long the Poles set up an elective monarchy which gave them weak kings and internal confusion. Once in a while a strong ruler would appear. One such was John Sobieski, a huge and remarkable man with an equally remarkable wife, who in 1683 drove the Turks back from Vienna, having previously subdued the Cossack riders of the Ukraine after a forced march of 150 miles.

Then came the period of "Sarmatism," that is, an artificial attempt by the Poles to live as their ancestors had done. The landed gentry spent their lives in feasting and hunting. Instead of being given food, the starving peasants were obliged to buy their landlord's badly brewed ale. At the same time, these landed noblemen were imitating France, led on perhaps by the fact that a Polish princess had married King Louis XV. Just a few years before the French Revolution, the Polish were trying to live as the French did at Versailles.

Two other Slavic peoples who flourished in the Middle Ages were the Bulgarians and the Serbs. At different times each of them set up an empire which dominated wide areas in the Balkans and was a force to which the West and Byzantium had to pay attention.

The Bulgars were not pure Slavs but were a Slavic people

whose blood was mixed with that of their Turko-Tatar conquerors. The common people were Slavs, but the rulers were Turko-Tatar. However, they all spoke Slavic.

Asperich was the first of these slit-eyed raiders. He crossed the Danube in 650. Still flaunting the horsetail-banner of the Asiatic nomads, he was then little more than the savage chieftain of a wild-riding marauder band.

But hardly more than 150 years later, his successor Krum ruled from Dacia to Macedonia.

Fierce as he was, Krum had not wanted battle to the death with the Byzantines. The risks were too great.

"Take what thou wilt and depart in peace," he told the Byzantine emperor when the latter had driven him into the mountains after sacking the Bulgar capital with such cruelty that even babies were tossed into threshing machines.

But Nicephorus refused—and then allowed himself to be trapped in a narrow pass.

"*Zdravista!* To your good health!" toasted Krum as he drank fiery wine from a cup made of the emperor's skull.

Boris, who succeeded Krum's grandson—he was the first Bulgar Christian, he later became a monk—together with Boris's son, Symeon, and a still later ruler, Samuel, extended their rule even farther. The Bulgar Empire now reached to the Adriatic.

The Bulgars now not only threatened the Byzantine Empire, they imitated it. Symeon actually took the title of Tsar as did his successors. *Khagan* was too barbaric. At their capital, Great Preslaw, there was Byzantine splendor, Byzantine learning, Byzantine art and architecture.

"Its buildings are mighty," said a visiting Byzantine monk.

Bulgars

"Its columns are all of marble. Its frescoes show the heavens with the stars, sun, and moon, the earth with the grasses and trees, the sea with its fishes. It is impossible to tell of it. You must see it for yourself."

Yet today Bulgaria is supposedly one of the most backward countries in Europe!

It was not until 1014 when Basil the Bulgarslayer crushed

Tsar Samuel's army, and after blinding fifteen thousand of his captives, sent them back to him, that Bulgar power was broken. Even at that there was a second Bulgar Empire which lasted from 1185 to 1358.

The medieval Serbian Empire also threatened the Byzantines and imitated them.

This empire began very modestly in 1168 when Stephen Nemanya, who was Grand *Zhupan* or High Prince of the Rascia (that is, Old Serbia), came down from his white limestone mountains, and with the assistance of his brother, Saint Sava, not only persuaded the mountaineer Slav tribesmen to stand together, but liberated the Serbs from Byzantine overlordship and acquired extensive territories in the south.

His son, Stephen Nemanya II (called "Stephen the First Crowned," because he was crowned by a papal legate and later by his uncle Saint Sava), consolidated his father's power.

But it was not until 1331 under Stephen Dushan that the Serbian Empire reached its apogee. Stephen was another great medieval monarch. Described as "the tallest of men of all times," he had a lean frame and coal-black eyes, and he was monumentally audacious. Not content as Symeon of Bulgaria had been with the mere title of Tsar, he proclaimed himself Emperor of the Serbs, the Greeks (the Byzantines), the Bulgars, and the Albanians. Then he set about to enforce this claim. He almost succeeded.

But Stephen did more than just lead conquering armies. His predecessors had built magnificent monasteries, such as those at Dečani and Gračenitsa and elsewhere in the remotest mountains. In these monasteries were mosaics which compared favorably with those in Constantinople and frescoes almost as good as those of the Italian painter Giotto. They had encouraged the shepherds and the swineherds. The sailors of Ragusa and Venice were fed with pork from the Rascia. They had reopened the copper, iron, gold, and silver mines which had been closed since the days of the Romans.

Stephen did one thing more. An enlightened monarch, he knew that military strength and wealth were not enough. There must be law and justice. From his court at Skoplje—when I saw it in 1924 Skoplje was a sleepy, almost Turkish town where fat men with red fezzes rode on little donkeys—he issued a new code which he called the *Zakonnik*. It combined old Slavic custom with Byzantine (and Roman) legal procedures. Some think that it is among the more important law codes ever drawn.

The last of the medieval Slavic states was the Russia of Kiev and of the sea of grass. It was from Kiev, you will remember, that Askold and Dir with their followers came when they attacked the God-guarded city.

(Kiev, of course, was not the only medieval Russian state. It was merely the most important one. There were other Russian states at Suzdal and Ryazan east of present-day Moscow, Novgorod in the far north, Galich—Galicia—in the Carpathian foothills, Chernigov and Pereyaslav near Kiev, and Tmutorokan on the Sea of Azov. Nor was its ruling dynasty descended from Askold and Dir but from Rurik, who ruled in Novgorod.)

It was founded in the ninth century or perhaps even earlier; was first a typical Slav city of wooden huts and palisades; then under Askold and Dir it became a pirate city; but after Vladimir had converted its inhabitants to Christianity, it was

Serbs

possibly the most splendid and important city between Constantinople and Cathay.

Thietmar of Merseberg—the same one who had noticed the
Slav princess who rode and drank like a warrior—reported
that Kiev had two hundred churches and eight markets. Some
people think that he may have exaggerated, but its Golden

Russians

Gates (built before 1054) were as fine as any medieval military architecture, and its Cathedral of Santa Sophia, modeled after Santa Sophia in Constantinople, was filled with priceless art and treasure. Other travelers noted the beautiful workmanship of its gold and silver ornaments. The crown of Vladimir Monomakh with its sable trimmings, filigree, pearls, emeralds, and rubies is an example. It is now in the Kremlin. Travelers also spoke of its illuminated manuscripts.

Many of these manuscripts were Byzantine and religious, but some were Russian, for it was at Kiev that Russian learning took its very first step. The monastery where old Sylvester wrote his vivid, if crude, chronicle was not far from Kiev.

It also goes without saying that it was an important trade center. Kiev was a middleman between fabled Samarkand from whence caravans went out to all the East, and the equally fabled Byzantine capital. There was a Russian quarter in Constantinople and a large group of Russian merchants there.

But Kiev was also the center of European defense against the steppe nomads. The latter now filled most of the lands to the south and southeast, and they were not civilized as the Khazars had become. They were tent-dwellers who lived on horseflesh and fermented mare's milk. From 865 to 1243, the Kievans took the lead in trying to stand them off. Sometimes they fought alone, but sometimes they were aided by the other Russian princes—all those Sviatoslavs, Vsyevolods (including Vsyevolod Big Nest, called this because he had nearly fifty children), Vladimirs, Igors, Olegs, and many others which anyone who studies Russian history of the period finds so difficult and hard to remember.

The slavs are conquered and then rise again

But not one of these Slavic nations lasted until modern times.

Kievan Russia was the first to fall to invaders from the East who were related, if not too closely, to the Patzinaks and the Polovtsi and the other steppe tribesmen it had long resisted.

Near the Gobi Desert in the shadow of the lofty Altai Mountains, there was born in 1157 to a refugee band of half-starving horse nomads, a baby with stringy black hair named by his father Temujin (piece of iron or maybe blacksmith), but whom we know as Genghiz Khan. By sheer determination, this Genghiz—who was to be one of the ablest and most ruthless conquerors of all time—shaped his people of sheep-herders, cattle raisers, and wild antelope hunters into the deadliest military weapon yet known. With it he conquered northern and central Asia from the Yellow Sea to the Caspian.

His sons and grandsons went even farther. One grandson was Kublai, whose Cathay was so vividly described by Marco Polo. Another grandson pressed toward the west. Destroying as they went, Batu and his Mongols—or Tatars as they were also called—reached the Adriatic in one direction and the plains of Poland in another.

They engulfed Kiev in the process.

"They took it and slew all the citizens," wrote Giovanni de Piano Carpini, a Franciscan monk who visited the place six years later (1246). "It was once a large and populous city, but now it is nothing."

All around, he continued, the land was strewn with skulls and human bones.

"Scarcely two hundred inhabitants remained, and these were kept in extreme bondage."

Having wrought this ruin, the nomad horsemen withdrew. But only to Sarai, Batu's capital. This was a city of mud-brick houses and endless lines of tents on the left bank of the Volga River not very far from modern Stalingrad. From it emanated all Tatar power. There the nomads became known as the Golden Horde.

The Golden Horde now assumed the overlordship not merely of Kiev but of every one of the numerous Russian principalities from Novgorod in the north to Galicia in the mountains of southern Poland. They maintained this over-lordship almost without interruption for almost two hundred years.

The next Slavic nation to disappear was ancient Serbia. It too was brought down by nomads from Asia. Actually they were the people whom today we call the Turks.

These were a branch of the same people who produced the Magyars (Hungarians) and the Bulgars (that is, the Bulgar ruling classes) and the Khazars (and the Patzinaks and the Polovtsi) and also, strangely enough, the distant Finns.

The Turks first put in an appearance in the eleventh century at the time the Seljuk Turks began attacking the Byzantine Empire. A hundred years later they actually took captive a Byzantine emperor on the shores of Lake Van in eastern Turkey. Then they overran much of Asia Minor.

But it was their cousins, the Ottoman Turks, who destroyed Serbia. The Ottomans are the Turks of present-day Turkey. When the Seljuks fell to the same Tatars who had destroyed Kiev, these Ottoman Turks took over Turkish leadership. In

1354, a Byzantine emperor foolishly invited them into Europe. They never again left. Within three decades half of the Balkans was in their hands.

It was at this time (1355) that Stephen Dushan died. With him went the Serbs' last chance. For he was succeeded by some very weak rulers. One of them, Prince Lazar—he did not dare call himself king, let alone emperor—tried frantically to organize a coalition of the now almost numberless Balkan states. He was at best half successful, and when his hodge-podge horde met the highly trained Ottoman army at Kosovo Polje ("The Field of Blackbirds," called this because so many crows came in to feast on the slain) on June 20, 1389, not even the murder of the sultan on the eve of the battle kept them from being utterly annihilated. Serb story blames the defeat on the treachery of Lazar's son-in-law, Vuk Branković, who goes down in history with Ganelon and Benedict Arnold. But this is merely national pride.

Bulgaria went down at almost the same time. Its last empire had disintegrated some thirty-one years earlier and the Turks hardly had to fight to win it. From then on, it became almost the most Turkish of Turkish *sanjaks* (provinces). There was even a whole class of Bulgars, the Pomaks, who were converted to Islam and helped the Turks oppress the Christian Bulgars. But that may have been because the Turks and the Bulgars were at least partly of the same race.

An independent Bohemia lasted for at least two centuries longer. It was destroyed not by invasion but by civil war.

Ever since the death of John Huss this sturdy nation in the heart of Europe had been torn by fierce warfare between the Catholics and the Protestants. And yet somehow it had managed to survive.

But early in the seventeenth century the conflict grew really bitter. The Catholics, who were then in power, closed two churches in two little Czech villages. In reprisal, the Czech Protestants threw two anti-Protestant ministers out of the windows of Prague castle. This is the famous "defenestration." Although they were not killed, savage fighting broke out, and on November 8, 1620, at the Battle of the White Mountain near Prague, the Czech Protestant nation was destroyed.

"Thou shalt break them with a rod of iron," cried the Spanish ambassador.

(Foreigners have always intervened in Czech affairs.)

Twenty-seven Czech leaders, including one eighty-six years old, were executed. Their faces grinned for ten years from the very Prague castle from which they had thrown the anti-Protestant ministers. Bohemia was attached to the Austrian Empire.

Poland lingered on even longer. But as you have already seen, its weak kings and wrangling nobility brought it closer and closer to disaster. Finally it was partitioned by its three strong neighbors. In 1772, again in 1793, and once more in 1795, Russia, Austria, and Prussia each gobbled up a tasty slice. When they had finished, Poland had disappeared.

But if they fell, the Slavic nations ultimately rose again—and in the very same order in which they had gone down.

Russia became a nation again first. When the Golden Horde withdrew to Sarai, the khan, as we have already seen, did not give up his claim to Russian tribute, and he also found it convenient to collect this tribute not through Tatar tax collectors but through a Russian ruler whom he would name Grand Prince. He also made it plain that he would choose this ruler and give him his new title. This he did.

But this Tatar khan was a shrewd man and so were his successors. Thus they did not choose for this important post a Russian prince whose state was already powerful.

In 1156, there had been founded at the junction of the Oka and the Moskva rivers a small settlement of very little significance.

It was known as Moskva, which means "troubled waters." We call it Moscow.

Because it was of very little significance and also centrally located, the khans thought it would be both safe and practical to trust its ruler.

One of these rulers was summoned from the Kremlin (walled fortress) to the Tatar tent city.

"From henceforward, you are Grand Prince of Muscovy."

But the khan also made it plain that this title would last only as long as taxes were forthcoming.

On that day, although no one realized it, modern Russia was born. For the Grand Princes of Moscow knew a good thing when they saw it, and they knew also how to take advantage of it.

Because they collected Tatar tribute, the Grand Princes were protected by the Tatars. "Let us make good use of this," they thought.

One after another these rulers brought the other Russian principalities under their control. In the end they even conquered and subdued mighty Novgorod. They deported its troublemaking (from a Muscovite point of view) ruling classes to central Russia. But that was not until 1478.

In the meantime, they slowly and cautiously moved against the Tatars themselves. Ivan Kalita—Ivan Moneybag (1325–1341)—lived up to his name. He bought immunity. But Dmitri Donskoi—Dmitri of the Don (1359–1389)—actually defeated the Golden Horde in battle. Final liberation came in the reign of Ivan the Great (1462–1505). Although the Tatars once marched the very walls of Moscow (1480), Ivan knew how to take advantage of the disunity which had now grown up among them. In the end the Crimea Tatars were even his allies.

It was Ivan the Great who established Russia as the most important Slav power, a position which it has never lost. He married Zoë, the niece of the last Byzantine emperor, and proclaimed himself Byzantium's heir. He proclaimed Moscow the Third Rome. He made Russia the protector of the Orthodox Church. He began to rebuild the Kremlin. Finally he called himself Tsar, although the title was not used formally for 75 years. This Ivan was the first of a line of tsars who reigned until 1917. They were all more or less related to each other.

(To be sure, Michael Romanov, founder of the house of Romanov, did not inherit the throne. He was elected to it in 1613 after the so-called "time of troubles" when one pretender after another claimed the throne, and the whole land was thrown into confusion. But at least Michael was the grandson of an earlier tsar's sister.)

There was Ivan the Terrible (1533–1584). Ivan slew his son with his own hands in a fit of mad fury. But he set up the first printing press east of Poland, gave Russia a national assembly, and welcomed English merchants like Sir Richard Chancellor whose description of Ivan "in a long garment of beaten gold with a staff of gold and crystal" is still worth reading. Ivan wanted to marry Queen Elizabeth. When she refused, he roared to the English ambassador that she was a low and ill-bred woman.

There was Peter the Great (sole ruler from 1689–1725). Peter was nearly seven feet tall, given to drinking too much, and happiest when he was surrounded by shipbuilders. He too killed his own son (or rather had him flogged to death), but not in a fit of temper. He killed him because Alexis was too reactionary. But under the assumed name of Peter Michaelovitch, a plain citizen, he traveled incognito to Germany, Holland, England, and other countries; and although he and his companions shocked the Westerners with their rowdy ways, he brought back a head full of ideas. It was he who built St. Petersburg and made it his capital. Moscow was too Russian.

There was Catherine I, a Lithuanian peasant girl, whom Peter took as his second wife and then taught to be a great empress.

There was Catherine the Great, a German princess who also became an outstanding Russian ruler. But Catherine was

Ivan the Terrible

gullible as well as great, and when her favorite, Potëmkin, wished to impress her he built a stage-set village on the banks of the Volga. Each day he moved it ahead of her. So she saw a succession of villages, all gay and prosperous.

There was Alexander I, who was first an ally of Napoleon and later helped defeat him. There is something very mysterious about Alexander. After a long reign he retired to the Crimea where he is supposed to have died. But many people believe that he did not die, but wandered off to Siberia where he became a monk.

Peter the Great

There was Alexander II. Alexander wanted to be known as the reformer tsar. He set free the serfs, established local self-government, and made everybody—instead of just the lower classes—liable for military service. But like most autocrat reformers he was never in touch with the people, and a terrorist bomb finally killed him.

Finally, there was poor Nicholas II. Nicholas was a weak man rather than a bad one, but he inherited the consequences of the foolishness and mismanagements of his predecessors. He was also subject to bad influences such as that of the wicked monk Rasputin, who perhaps more than anyone else was responsible for the Russian revolution. Nicholas and his whole family were brutally murdered by the Bolsheviks (today we call them Communists). At his death the Russian imperial line ended.

Serbia was the second Slav nation to gain its independence.

(Unless you count Montenegro, that is. This mountaineer state, long governed by *vladikas,* or prince-bishops, says that it *never* yielded to the Turks. It was absorbed into Yugoslavia in 1918.)

After Kosovo, the inhabitants of Serbia had either been converted to Islam (even today there are several million Moslem Serbs) in which case they enjoyed full Turkish privileges, or reduced to the status of a *rayah,* or brutally taxed peasant. Every rayah had to pay a crushing tax whenever the Turks wanted it. Serbian sons were taken for the Turkish army. Serbian daughters went to Turkish harems.

But deep in the forests and the mountains, there still lingered the spirit of freedom, and in 1804, a rich swine-raiser—he was originally named George Petrović, but was known as

Karageorge, or Black George—raised the banner of revolt. For a while he was successful, but he was a moody man (he had once hanged his own brother—for a crime, to be sure, but without any trial) and in a moment of despair, he fled the country. Another Serb, Miloš Obrenovich, then assumed Serb leadership, and it was he who actually broke Turkish rule. Indeed, the sultan himself recognized Miloš as Prince of Serbia. The Serbians have been independent ever since.

(Incidentally, the Karageorgevichs—the descendants of Black George—and the Obrenovichs have been feuding for almost as long as there has been a modern Serbia. They murdered each other with ruthless regularity, and when they did not murder, they plotted and intrigued. There have been five rulers of the Obrenovich family and four of the Karageorgevich family. The last king was a Karageorgevich.)

Bulgaria became at least nominally independent in 1878. Since this was largely with Russian assistance, her early days were checkered. The other powers, especially France and England, did not want Russian influence too deep in the Balkans. Even today Bulgaria is the least important of the Slavic countries.

Czechoslovakia (the former Bohemia) and Poland did not again become nations until World War I.

Indeed, the Czechs and the Czech language—like the Irish language—almost disappeared. They and it were kept alive only by the efforts of Czech scholars who, oppressed though they were by Austria, somehow preserved the Czech spirit. As a matter of fact the modern state of Czechoslovakia was called into being by a group of Czech intellectuals who met in the United States. The first Czech government was set up in Paris.

Ignace Paderewski

The Poles also refounded their state with American help and under Allied influence. But Poland had never quite disappeared. There was always strong Polish national feeling even when there was no Polish nation. A Pole, Adam Czartoryski, actually became Prime Minister of Russia, in hopes of freeing Poland. At one time there was even a Kingdom of Poland under the Russian tsar.

But when the new Polish state was set up—like Czechoslovakia but unlike the Serbs, the Yugoslavs, and Bulgaria (which were ruled by princes, kings, and even a tsar)— it was a republic with a president and a prime minister and a parliament, the *Sejm*.

Strangely enough, the first prime minister was the world-famous pianist, Ignace Jan Paderewski. He took office in January, 1919.

Imagine that! Not a general or a lawyer or a financier or a professor of government or a leader of the peasants or of the workers, but a renowned musician! It was Paderewski's lectures, his piano-playing, and his popularity which had made Poland free as much as anything else.

Besides that he was the prime minister of a Slavic country, not a Latin or a German or an Anglo-Saxon one.

And imagination—daring, if not always practical imagination—is one of the most important characteristics of the Slav.

WhAT The slavs
haVe Done foR us

Besides imagination, what other characteristics do the Slavic people have?

What, for example, has little Pyotr of Russia inherited from his long line of ancestors who have climbed from their primitive marshes? His father manufactures tractors or atomic warheads in the Donets basin or at Novosibirsk beyond the Ural Mountains.

Or Stoyan of Yugoslavia, who, in spite of his country's new concentration on industry, still herds his sheep from their summer pastures in the mountains to warm valleys where they will spend the winter as his grandfather and his grandfather's grandfather had herded them before him?

(But Stoyan's uncle used to be one of the *pechalbari*—workers who left home for a year or more, sometimes traveling as far as America and returning with their earnings.)

Or Václav of Prague?

Or little Georgi from the Bulgarian Maritsa Valley with its olive trees and its tobacco?

105

Or Wladyslaw from some little Polish farm town with its single-story houses and straw roofs?

What have the Slavs done with these characteristics?

What may they do again?

After World War I, in a book called *Who Are the Slavs?* which he wrote in the United States, an exiled Russian professor tried to give some of the answers. It is worth listening to what he had to say.

"The Slav," he began, "is melancholy. He is melancholy and sad.

"The Slav is patient and long suffering.

" 'What does life mean to us?' say the Slav peasants. 'A feast? No! Work? Not even work! A battle? Not a battle! Merely a heavy burden. Only after grinding will come flour. Christ suffered in patience. So must we.'

"The Slav is filled with love and sympathy.

"He calls his father little father, his brother little brother, and his sweetheart little pigeon. All people are of one blood and one race, the Slav says.

"The Slav is humble and lacks hypocrisy.

"However, the Slav is indecisive. That is because he is a fatalist.

"The Slav also loves paradoxes. The same man will go into a mystical trance or order a pogrom."

This is what a Slav says about the Slavs, but Professor Radosavlyevich had some other observations to make, and they too are worth our attention.

"The ancient chronicles call this people industrious, peaceful and obedient. They tell us that they made war only in self defense. These ancient writers also show us that even before they had a history, the Slavs loved poetry and music. 'They lull themselves to sleep with their eternal songs,' wrote Constantine Born-in-the-Purple. The Slavs, they pointed out finally, had an intense feeling of nationality. 'Who can resist God—or Lord Novgorod?' was another Slav saying.

"The modern Slav," Professor Radosavlyevich continued, "has these qualities and some others as well. He is strong, prolific, capable of long suffering if he believes the cause to be right, thrifty, hard-working, religious, and moral.

"The Bulgar is particularly attentive to business. To be sure, he is often cold-blooded and calculating. But that comes from his Asiatic background.

"The Serb does not have the Bulgar's business ability, but he is loyal, charming, and simple to deal with. However, he is impulsive, tempestuous, and sensitive. He is very brave. The Serb is cheerful too."

For a Slav, that is!

"He loves a practical joke. He loves to sing and dance and laugh. He loves to hear—or, better, to tell—a good story.

"The Czech is intelligent, but he is proud and argumentative. He is orderly, gentle, and trustworthy. He is apt to have business ability—but not of the shrewd, bazaar-bargaining kind the Bulgar has. He is not as inflammable as the Slavs to the north and the south. But he never forgets an injury.

"The Pole is more romantic than the other Slavs. He loves political freedom almost to the point of anarchy, but he is easily captured by the pomp and glitter of a throne. More often than not, he is a poor businessman, but he has great intellectual ability and he can learn almost any language. He is brave and brilliant but he is politically unsuccessful."

A Russian himself, the professor said less about the Russians, but he did point out that the Russian people too are long-suffering and slow to wrath, but from time to time they rise in fury. Although they seem stolid and apathetic, circumstances can transform them into fiery apostles or models of disciplined control.

Indeed, he left out only one Slav characteristic. The Slav is extremely adaptable.

"The Slav," said a famous Slavic writer, "is the red-hot iron between the German anvil and the Tatar hammer."

By this he meant that throughout their history the Slavs have either fought off or absorbed invasions from both east and west. That they have been the buffer which has protected both Europe and Asia from would-be world conquerors.

But he could have meant just as well that they had been hammered out and shaped by both eastern and western influences. Not merely either by the Tatars and the Germans. By the Byzantines. By the Italians. By the French (in Poland anyway) and by the English. Even by the Arabs and the Persians.

That if they have been this buffer in the area of world conquest and world domination, in the area of the mind and of the spirit, they have also been a link between two worlds.

It is these qualities and these influences that have been responsible for all the Slavs have done and accomplished, and this has been a very great deal.

It is Slavic patience and long suffering, for instance, that kept the Slavs true to their Slavic heritage during years and even centuries of oppression and tyranny. (Sometimes by the Turks and Tatars, but quite often by their fellow Slavs.)

Copernicus

It is their courage and their sense of nationality that have made them rise again.

It is their thrift and innate peasant shrewdness that have enabled them to survive both their incredibly harsh climate and an equally harsh misrule.

But it is in the realm of the imagination that they have made their biggest contribution, and nowhere is this more apparent than in Slavic folk achievement.

When Professor Radosavlyevich was discussing the drab Slavic countryside, he said: "The only brilliant coloring is in the dress of the peasants."

Anybody who has ever gone to any Slav country knows that this is true. The Slav peasant costume with its embroidery, its white starch, its brilliant blues and reds, is like nothing else in the world. Not long ago, these costumes were all made of cloth woven on home looms; and the embroidery was sewn at night by oil light, candle, or even the fire. It was virtual slavery for the women, but it was the art expression of the people.

Many of the world's most famous fairy stories are Slavic, including "The Twelve Months," about Maruša and her wicked stepmother, which is the Czech version of Cinderella. But instead of marrying a prince and moving into the palace, Maruša inherits a cottage and a cow!

Slavic dances—whether the wild Russian sword dance or the more sober Serbian kolo where men and women move slowly in a circle—lie at the back of most of our ballet.

But perhaps the greatest Slav folk achievement was the Slavic folk ballad. The Russians had their *Song of the Sword of Igor* about the campaigns against the Cumans and Polovtsi.

Anton Dvořák

You can read it in an English translation. But even greater were the Serb Kosovo poems.

After that terrible defeat, unknown minstrels composed a series of ballads about the battle, and they were combined into a folk epic. It was sung by *guslars,* or bards, called this because they accompanied their words with a *gusle,* or one-stringed violin.

This is how it began:

> In the old palace of Kruchevac the white,
> The Lord of Serbia, the Serbian Prince Lazar,
> All his free-hearted princes did unite.
> Behold two hundred of them there that night there are!

Then it went on to tell the story of the battle and the men who fought it. It told of the traitor Vuk Branković, "with the eyes that shift"; of Yug Bogdan with his nine stout sons; of the fair Melitsa, Yug's daughter and Lazar's wife; and for the hero Miloš Obelich who slew the sultan.

During the long years when they were ruled by the Turks, there was hardly a Serb who did not know the epic by heart. Actually, it kept alive the Serb spirit. Even more than Serbia's warriors, more than Karageorge and Miloš Obrenovich, it set the nation free.

But the Slavs had their formal accomplishments in the realm of imagination, too, and these are best shown to you by setting down a few great names.

In science, in addition to Copernicus there was Madame Curie, who discovered radium; Mendeleyev who found out that the elements could be arranged in orderly rows, each with its own properties. Mendeleyev's discovery made possible not only Madame Curie's contributions but those of every other atomic researcher.

Among patriots and great generals there was not only John Sobieski and John Žižka; but Alexander Nevski who in the Middle Ages threw back the Swedes; Thaddeus Kosciusko and Count Casimir Pulaski, both of whom, after failing to keep their own country free, helped the Colonies win the

Leo Tolstoy

American Revolution. Why, Scanderbeg, the great fifteenth-century Albanian hero, was of Slavic origin.

In art, there were not merely the anonymous builders of the Kremlin—with its Oriental color, its Byzantine gold, and its purely Russian onion-shaped towers—and the anonymous artists of mosaics and frescoes in old monasteries in Serbia and Bulgaria. There was the Yugoslav Ivan Meštrović, one of the greatest sculptors since the Renaissance. He died in the United States in 1962.

In letters, there is not merely Tolstoy whose *War and Peace* is often considered the greatest novel ever written. Tolstoy was also one who, at his villa at Yasnaya Polyana (Bright

Field), taught love and purity. There was Dostoevski, who wrote *Crime and Punishment,* and Gogol with his *Dead Souls* and Henry Sienkiewicz, who wrote *Quo Vadis?* and Boris Pasternak. Even Joseph Conrad, the English writer of sea tales, was originally a Slav. He was born Teodor Józef Konrad Korzeniowski in a little inland Polish village.

In music, there was Chopin and Anton Dvořák and Rimski-Korsakov and Tchaikovsky and Scriabin and Moussorgsky. But the Slavs have contributed to popular music too. The gay dance rhythms of Poland's polkas and mazurkas are known all over the world.

I could go on and on.

Today, of course, the Slavs are no longer living in a world which makes such achievements likely or perhaps even possible, for since World War II every single Slavic nation or state has fallen into Communist hands. The Slavs are being taught to regard as enemies the free world which has admired and respected them, and to distrust the freedom of the mind which made many of their achievements possible. This goes for the democratic Czechs, the liberty-loving Poles, and the hospitable and fiercely patriotic Yugoslavs, just as much as it does for the Russians and the hapless Bulgarians. But no absolute rule lasts forever, and this should be particularly true among the tenacious Slavs. One day they will surely be free again, and then once more each and every one of them will be able to take charge of his own destiny.

In that day, they will resume the march which has already carried them so far.

CHRONOLOGICAL CHART OF
SLAVIC HISTORY
AND WORLD EVENTS

BOOKS FOR FURTHER READING

INDEX AND GLOSSARY

SLAVIC PEOPLES				
POLAND	CZECHOSLOVAKIA	YUGOSLAVIA	BULGARIA	RUSSIA

First Slavs settle in central Europe, after 2500 B.C.; further migrations east, west, south, southeast, and southwest (Slavic clans and tribes begin unification into nations), about 700–800 A.D.

	POLAND	CZECHOSLOVAKIA	YUGOSLAVIA	BULGARIA	RUSSIA
A.D. 600–700		Earliest known Slavic kingdom under Samo, 631–659: Occupies almost all S central Europe		Nomadic Bulgars subjugate Slavic tribes, about 650	
700–800		Legendary founding of first Czech dynasty by Libuša and Přemysl, 8th century–1306 Legendary founding of Prague			
800–900	Legendary founding of first Polish dynasty under Piast, about 850–1370	Introduction of Christianity, about 870		Krum subdues Byzantines; rules from Dacia to Macedonia, about 800 Boris I, 853–888 Introduction of Christianity, about 870 Symeon, 893–927: First Tsar of Bulgaria First Bulgarian Empire attains greatest power, extends to Adriatic Capital at Great Preslav; center of Byzantine art and learning	Rurik establishes first Russian state at Novgorod, about 855 Invasion of Constantinople under vikings, 860 Capital moved to Kiev, about 880
900–1000	Mieszko introduces Christianity, about 960				Vladimir makes Christianity state religion, about 990
1000–1100		Acquisition of Moravia		Byzantines under Basil defeat Bulgarians, 1014	Kiev becomes center of trade, learning, and defense Raids by Polovtsi and other steppe nomads
1100–1200			Stephen Nemanya I liberates Serbs from Byzantine control, 1168; extensive territories in south acquired Stephen Nemanya II consolidates Serbian power	Second Bulgarian Empire, 1185–1358	Moscow founded, 1156
1200–1300					Tatars under Batu Khan destroy Kiev, 1240: Golden Horde established in S and E Russia, 1240–1480
1300–1400	Casimir III, 1333–1370	Charles I (Charles IV), 1347–1378: Golden Age of Bohemia	Stephen Dushan, 1331: Serbian Empire at peak		Novgorod important trade center

	ENGLAND AND WESTERN EUROPE	NEAR EAST AND ASIA	WESTERN HEMISPHERE
	Folk wandering; migrations of peoples in borderlands of Europe; throughout almost all of Asia north of Himalayas, about 200 A.D.– 1000 A.D.		
A.D. 600–700		Beginning of Arab Empire, 632; Arabs conquer Persia, Egypt, North Africa, Spain	Maya period of prosperity, 300–700
700–800	(Charles Martel defeats Moslems at Tours, France, 732; stops Arab expansion in Europe)		
800–900	Charlemagne crowned emperor of Holy Roman Empire at Rome, 800	Golden Age of Arab Empire under Abbasid dynasty, 750–1258	
		Constantinople invaded by vikings, 860	
		Byzantine civilization advances greatly under Macedonian dynasty, 867–1056	
900–1000	(Arab rule in Spain at height: Cordova greatest intellectual center in western Europe)		Eric the Red discovers Greenland, about 985
1000–1100	William the Conqueror invades England, 1066	Seljuk Turks seize Baghdad, 1055; defeat Byzantines in Armenia, 1071 (decline of Byzantine military power) Raids by Patzinaks, Polovtsi, etc., into Russia	Leif Ericson visits Vinland, about 1000
1100–1200	(Crusades against Moslems in Holy Lands, 1096–1270)		
1200–1300	Magna Charta in England, 1215	Genghis Khan conquers all of central Asia and China, 1206–1221	
1300–1400		Mongols destroy Baghdad and overthrow Arab Empire, 1258 Marco Polo in Far East, 1271–1295 Ottoman Turks found empire, 1288	

	SLAVIC PEOPLES				
	POLAND	CZECHOSLOVAKIA	YUGOSLAVIA	BULGARIA	RUSSIA
	Growth of national defense	Prague cultural center of central Europe; founding of University of Prague, 1348	Introduction of law code		Ivan Kalita, 1328–1341
	Promotion of trade, industry	John Žižka, 1360?–1424	(Bulgars become tributary to Serbia)		Foundation of Muscovite kingdom: Beginning of modern Russian state
	University of Kraków founded	John Huss, 1369?–1415	Much of Byzantium conquered; introducing Byzantine culture		
	Jagellon dynasty, 1386–1572: Golden Age of medieval Poland Intellectual center of western Europe		Succession of weak rulers, 1355–1398		Dmitri Donskoi. 1359–1389
			Defeat by Ottoman Turks at Kosovo Polje, 1389	Turks absorb Bulgars after Kosovo Polje, 1389	Subdues Tatars, establishing Muscovite power, 1380
1400–1500	Combined territory of Poland, Lithuania reaches peak: Extends to Black Sea, including most of W Russia, and reaches Baltic	Hussite War, 1419–1434	Serbia annexed by Turks, 1459		Ivan the Great, 1462–1505: End of Tatar domination, 1480
					Russia established as most important Slav power Russia proclaimed protector of Orthodox Eastern Church Moscow proclaimed "Third Rome" Kremlin rebuilt
1500–1600			[Montenegrins under prince-bishops continue resistance to Turks, 1516–1851]		
	Power of kings declines; internal confusion in government				Ivan the Terrible, 1533–1584 First national assembly, 1556
1600–1700		Thirty Years' War, 1618–1648			Romanov dynasty, 1613–1917
	John Sobieski drives Turks back from Vienna, 1683 Weak government continues	Czech Protestant nation destroyed, 1620			Peter the Great, 1689–1725

	ENGLAND AND WESTERN EUROPE	NEAR EAST AND ASIA	WESTERN HEMISPHERE
	(Tamerlane ruler of Asia from Russia to Persian Gulf, 1369–1405)		
	(Ottoman Turks invade Europe, defeat Serbs, 1389: Byzantine Empire suffers greatly)		
1400–1500	Renaissance	Ottoman Turks overthrow Byzantine Empire, 1453; control Arabs, 1453–1923: Blocking of trade routes to Far East	Rise of Aztec civilization
	Invention of printing by movable type, 1439		
	Moors expelled from Spain: Beginning of Spanish explorations in New World		Columbus discovers America, 1492
1500–1600	Martin Luther and rise of Protestantism		Aztec and Inca civilization at height
	(Ottoman Turks control lands of SE Europe, W Asia, and N Africa)		
	(Magellan voyages around the world, 1519–1522 ————————————→)		
	(Turkish expanison into Europe stopped at Vienna, 1529)		
	Elizabeth I in England, 1558–1603		Cortes conquers Mexico, 1519–1521: Pizarro conquers Peru, 1531–1535
	Defeat of Spanish Armada, 1588; England gains control of seas		
1600–1700	Thirty Years' War in central Europe, 1618–1648: Holy Roman Empire becomes minor factor in European politics	Manchu Dynasty in China, 1644–1912	Pilgrims land at Plymouth, 1620
	(Turks driven back from Vienna, 1683; Turkish power diminished by Treaty of Karlowitz, 1699)		

SLAVIC PEOPLES				
POLAND	CZECHOSLOVAKIA	YUGOSLAVIA	BULGARIA	RUSSIA

	POLAND	CZECHOSLOVAKIA	YUGOSLAVIA	BULGARIA	RUSSIA
1700–1800		Bohemia becomes crownland of Austrian Hapsburgs, 1627			Introduced Western culture: Russia begins to be one of great European powers St. Petersburg founded as capital, 1703 Catherine the Great, 1762–1796 Large conquests extend empire Partitions of Poland, 1772, 1793, 1795
1800–1900	Partitions of Poland by Russia, Austria, Prussia, 1772, 1793, 1795: Poland disappears		Karogeorge leads revolution against Turks, 1804 Miloš founds Obrenovich dynasty, 1817: Recognition by Turks, 1828 Serbia and Montenegro independent after Congress of Berlin, 1878	Bulgaria becomes principality after Congress of Berlin, 1878	Crimea annexed, 1783 Russia replaces Austria as chief enemy of Turks Russia defeats Turkey, 1877–1878: Serious diplomatic reverses after Congress of Berlin, 1878 Nicholas II, 1894–1917
1900–	Poland becomes independent republic, 1918	Czechoslovakia becomes independent republic, 1918	Serbia and Montenegro unified in Kingdom of Serbs, Croats, and Slovenes, 1918 (name changes to Yugoslavia, 1929)	Bulgaria becomes independent kingdom, 1908 Loss of territory after W.W.I.	Russian Revolution by Bolshevik Communists, 1917: End of Russian imperial line U.S.S.R. established, 1922
	Partition by Germany and U.S.S.R., 1939 Poland becomes Soviet-modeled "people's democracy," 1947		W.W.II: Tito's Communists merge with royal government, 1944 Federal People's Republic created, 1945: Serbia, Croatia, Bosnia and Hercegovina, Macedonia, and Montenegro created as autonomous people's republics, 1946	Monarchy abolished, 1946: Establishment of republic under Communists	U.S.S.R. in W.W.II, 1941–1945 Cominform established, 1947
		Communists take over government, 1948	Yugoslavia expelled from Cominform, 1948		

ISTORY AND WORLD EVENTS

	ENGLAND AND WESTERN EUROPE	NEAR EAST AND ASIA	WESTERN HEMISPHERE
1700–1800	Beginning of Industrial Revolution		
	(War between England and France takes place in Europe, India, and America, 1754–1763)		
	French Revolution, 1788–1799		American Revolution, 1775–1783
	Partitions of Poland, 1772, 1793, 1795		Declaration of Independence, 1776
1800–1900	Napoleon defeated at Waterloo, 1815		
			Mexico wins independence from Spain, 1821
	Formation of Austro-Hungarian Empire, 1867		Civil War in U.S., 1861–1865
1900–	(Suez Canal, 1869, opens shorter trade route to E Asia: European empires established throughout Asia and Africa)		Wrights' first plane flight, 1903
		Chinese Revolution, 1911–1912: Manchu Dynasty overthrown	
	W.W.I, 1914–1918		U.S. enters W.W.I, 1917
	W.W.II, 1939–1945: Germany suffers defeat and occupation by U.S., France, Great Britain, U.S.S.R.	End of Turkish Empire in Near East, 1923: Creation of independent Arab States, 1930–1945 Japan defeated in W.W.II	U.S. enters W.W.II, 1941
			First successful atom bomb test at Alamogordo, New Mexico, 1945
		State of Israel established, 1948	

BOOKS FOR FURTHER READING

Adamic, Louis, *The Native's Return* (Yugoslavia). New York, Harper & Brothers, 1934.

Baudiš, Josef, *Czech Folk Tales*. London, G. Allen & Unwin, Ltd., 1917.

Crew, Helen Coale, *Under Two Eagles* (Poland). Boston, Little, Brown & Company, 1929.

Čurčija-Prodanović, Nada, *Yugoslav Folk-Tales*. London, Oxford University Press, 1957.

Dvornik, Francis, *The Slavs: Their Early History and Civilization*. Boston, American Academy of Arts and Sciences, 1956.

Gronowicz, Antoni, *The Piasts of Poland*. New York, Charles Scribner's Sons, 1945.

Houghton, Louise Seymour, *The Russian Grandmother's Wonder Tales*. New York, Charles Scribner's Sons, 1906.

Jarecka, Louise Llewellyn, *Made in Poland*. New York, Alfred A. Knopf, 1949.

Kellogg, Charlotte, *Jadwiga, Poland's Great Queen*. New York, The Macmillan Company, 1931.

Kelly, Eric P., *From Star to Star* (Poland). Philadelphia and New York, J. B. Lippincott Company, 1944.

———, *Trumpeter of Krakow*. New York, The Macmillan Company, 1928.

Lamb, Harold, *The City and the Tsar* (Russia). Garden City, Doubleday & Company, Inc., 1948.

———, *The March of Muscovy* (Russia). Garden City, Doubleday & Company, Inc., 1948.

Nazaroff, Alexander, *The Land of the Russian People*. New York, Alfred A. Knopf, 1953.

Pribichevich, Stoyan, *World Without End* (Czechoslovakia). New York, Reynal & Hitchcock, 1939.

Runciman, Steven, *The First Bulgarian Empire.* London, Bell Publishers, 1930.

Strakhovsky, Leonid Ivanovich, ed., *Handbook of Slavic Studies.* Cambridge, Harvard University Press, 1949.

Vernadsky, George, *History of Russia.* New London, Yale University Press (Y43), 1961.

West, Rebecca, *Black Lamb and Grey Falcon* (Yugoslavia). New York, The Viking Press, 1941.

INDEX AND GLOSSARY